Contents

GRANDPA'S POPCORN BALLS 5

MICROWAVE PRALINES 6

HARD CANDY 6

CARAMELS 7

GERMAN CHOCOLATE FUDGE 7

EMILY'S FAMOUS MARSHMALLOWS 8

CARAMEL CORN 9

WHITE CHOCOLATE COVERED PRETZELS 9

BOARDWALK QUALITY MAPLE WALNUT FUDGE 10

LAYERED MINT CHOCOLATE FUDGE 10

CANDIED APPLES 11

PEANUT BUTTER FUDGE 11

CINNAMON-SUGAR POPCORN 12

PEANUT BUTTER CANDY BARS 13

CARAMEL PEANUT FUDGE 13

KENTUCKY BOURBON BALLS 14

SPOOKY HALLOWEEN EYEBALLS 15

ALMOND CRUNCH 15

RASPBERRY TRUFFLE FUDGE 16

LAYERED PEPPERMINT BARK 17

HARD ROCK CANDY 17

QUEIJADAS 18

SODA CRACKER CANDY 18

ROCKY ROAD CANDIES 19

BASIC TRUFFLES 19

WHITE CHOCOLATE FUDGE 20

ORANGE CREAM FUDGE 20

EASTER EGGS 21

FROSTED CRANBERRIES 22

MAGIC WANDS 22

CHOCOLATE COVERED CARAMELS 23

ANGEL FOOD CANDY 23

CHOCOLATE WALNUT FUDGE 24

EAGLE BRAND PEANUT BUTTER FUDGE 24

GRANDMA'S PEANUT BUTTER FUDGE 25

EASY TOFFEE 25

PURE MAPLE CANDY 26

CHOCOLATE COVERED EASTER EGGS 26

OLD-FASHIONED DIVINITY CANDY 27

ACORN CANDY COOKIES 28

EASY MICROWAVE PEANUT BRITTLE 28

JELLY BEAN NESTS 29

CHOCOLATE COVERED PEPPERMINT PATTIES 29

GOURMET CARAMEL APPLES 30

CHOCOLATE POPCORN 31

CRISPY RICE CANDY 31

PEANUT CLUSTERS 32

HALLOWEEN POPCORN PUMPKINS 32

WORLD'S BEST OREO FUDGE 33

SWEET CANDIED ORANGE AND LEMON PEEL 34

EASY VEGAN PEANUT BUTTER FUDGE 34

HAROSET FOR PASSOVER 35

GELATIN-FLAVORED POPCORN 35

NEVER-NEVER EVER-EVER FAIL FUDGE 36

CANDIED LEMON PEEL 36

FAT PETE'S FUDGE 37

CHOCOLATE ORANGE TRUFFLES 37

CHOCOLATE SPIDERS 38

CHOCOLATE-PEANUT BUTTER KETO CUPS 38

CHOCOLATE COVERED MARSHMALLOWS 39

PEPPERMINT MARSHMALLOWS 39

CATHY'S PEANUT BUTTER FUDGE 40

AMAZING HEALTHY DARK CHOCOLATE 41

SOFT CARAMEL CORN 41

MINT CHOCOLATE FUDGE 42

CANDY BAR FUDGE 42

ESPRESSO BARK 43

CREAM CHEESE CANDIES 44

SWEETENED POPCORN 44

LIP-SMACKING POPCORN CONCOCTION 45

PEPPERMINT BARK 45

JELLYBEAN BARK 46

CHOCOLATE PRETZEL TREATS 46

PEANUT BUTTER FUDGE WITH MARSHMALLOW CREME 47

PEANUT BUTTER CUPS 47

FAMOUS COCONUT-ALMOND BALLS 48

GA GA CLUSTERS 48

EASY MICROWAVE PRALINES 49

CARAMEL CANDIES 49

CREAMY EGGNOG FUDGE 50

BROWN SUGAR FUDGE 50

TIGER BUTTER 51

EASY CINNAMON FUDGE 51

CHOCOLATE COVERED CHERRIES 52

HOMEMADE MARSHMALLOWS 53

SWEDISH CHOCOLATE BALLS (OR COCONUT BALLS) 53

GOURMET PRETZEL RODS 54

PEANUT BUTTER POTATO CANDY 54

S'MORES 55

CRISPY MARSHMALLOW BALLS 55

CARAMEL CHOCOLATE CORN 56

EGGNOG FUDGE 57

NAT'S BUTTERY CASHEW CRUNCH 57

BAVARIAN MINTS 58

LICORICE CARAMELS 58

CHOCOLATE ORANGE FUDGE 59

EASTER EGG NESTS 59

ALMOND BUTTERCRUNCH CANDY 60

BRANDY OR RUM BALLS 61

ELISA'S FAMOUS FUDGE 61

OLD-FASHIONED PEANUT BRITTLE 62

TEXAS PRALINES 62

PRETZEL SMOOCHIES 63

CARAMEL POPCORN WITH MARSHMALLOW 63

CARAMEL CORN TREAT BAGS 64

GRAMMA'S EASY PEANUT BUTTER FUDGE 65

CHOCOLATE ALMOND BARK 65

FUDGE BONBONS 66

CARAMEL FOR APPLES 66

MORGAN'S AMAZING PEPPERMINT BARK 67

CHERRIES AND CHOCOLATE FUDGE 67

NEVER-FAIL FUDGE 68

CHOCOLATE PEANUT BUTTER CHIP FUDGE 68

WHITE CHOCOLATE GRAPES 69

CHINESE NEW YEAR CHOCOLATE CANDY 69

HOMEMADE MARSHMALLOWS 70

CANDIED CITRUS PEEL 70

CREAMY ORANGE FUDGE 71

MARIAN'S FUDGE 71

SUCRE A LA CREME 72

EASTER BIRD'S NESTS 72

INGREDIENT PEANUT BUTTER FUDGE 73

PEANUT BUTTER BON-BONS 73

STATE FAIR KETTLE CORN 74

CHERRY-PISTACHIO BARK 75

TOLL HOUSE FAMOUS FUDGE 75

COCONUT ICE 76

WALNUT MAPLE FUDGE 76

EASY CASHEW SEA SALT TOFFEE 77

CHEF JOHN'S CHRISTMAS MIRACLE FUDGE 78

BUTTERSCOTCH CANDY 78

DELICIOUS MATZO CANDY 79

CHOCOLATE COVERED POTATO CHIPS 80

A PEANUTTY S'MORE 80

OLD FASHIONED FUDGE 81

GRANDMA'S TAFFY 81

COCONUT BRITTLE 82

SIMPLE MICROWAVE PEANUT BRITTLE 83

QUICK NARIYAL BURFI (INDIAN COCONUT FUDGE) 83

OLD FASHIONED HARD CANDY 84

REINDEER POOP 84

HOMEMADE CARAMELS 85

PENUCHE 85

RUM TRUFFLES 86

MADE-IN-MINUTES NO-COOK FUDGE 87

CHOCOLATE COVERED BLUEBERRIES 87

LIQUOR-INFUSED CHOCOLATE STRAWBERRIES 88

TURTLES CANDY 88

MICROWAVE PECAN BRITTLE 89

BAKED FUDGE 90

CARROT RECIPE 90

GRANDPA'S POPCORN BALLS
Servings: 10 | Prep: 10m | Cooks: 15m | Total: 25m

NUTRITION FACTS

Calories: 458 | Carbohydrates: 75.1g | Fat: 18.7g | Protein: 1.7g | Cholesterol: 24mg

INGREDIENTS

- 2 cups white sugar
- salt to taste
- 1 cup light corn syrup
- 1 teaspoon vanilla extract
- 1/2 cup butter
- 1 teaspoon distilled white vinegar (optional)
- 1/4 cup water
- 5 quarts popped popcorn

DIRECTIONS

1. In a saucepan over medium heat, combine the sugar, corn syrup, butter and water. Stir and heat to hard-crack stage or 300 degrees F (150 degrees C). Remove from heat, add vanilla or vinegar; mix well.
2. Pour slowly over popped popcorn while stirring. Wait 5 minutes and shape into 3 inch round balls.

MICROWAVE PRALINES
Servings: 36 | Prep: 9m | Cooks: 9m | Total: 18m

NUTRITION FACTS

Calories: 87 | Carbohydrates: 9.8g | Fat: 5.4g | Protein: 0.5g | Cholesterol: 6mg

INGREDIENTS

- 1 1/2 cups brown sugar
- 2 tablespoons margarine
- 2/3 cup heavy cream
- 1 1/2 cups pecan halves
- 1/8 teaspoon salt
- 1 teaspoon vanilla extract

DIRECTIONS

1. In a large, microwave safe bowl, combine sugar, cream, salt, margarine and pecans. Microwave 9 minutes on high, stirring once. Let rest 1 minute. Stir in vanilla and continue to stir 3 minutes more. Drop by teaspoonfuls onto buttered waxed paper. (If mixture is runny, allow to cool 30 seconds more and try again.)

HARD CANDY
Servings: 36 | Prep: 5m | Cooks: 25m | Total: 45m

NUTRITION FACTS

Calories: 124 | Carbohydrates: 32.2g | Fat: 0g | Protein: 0g | Cholesterol: 0mg

INGREDIENTS

- 3 3/4 cups white sugar
- 1 tablespoon orange, or other flavored extract
- 1 1/2 cups light corn syrup
- 1/2 teaspoon food coloring (optional)
- 1 cup water
- 1/4 cup confectioners' sugar for dusting

DIRECTIONS

1. In a medium saucepan, stir together the white sugar, corn syrup, and water. Cook, stirring, over medium heat until sugar dissolves, then bring to a boil. Without stirring, heat to 300 to 310 degrees F (149 to 154 degrees C), or until a small amount of syrup dropped into cold water forms hard, brittle threads.
2. Remove from heat and stir in flavored extract and food coloring, if desired. Pour onto a greased cookie sheet, and dust the top with confectioners' sugar. Let cool, and break into pieces. Store in an airtight container.

CARAMELS
Servings: 117 | Prep: 45m | Cooks: 45m | Total: 1h30m

NUTRITION FACTS

Calories: 53 | Carbohydrates: 6.8g | Fat: 3.1g | Protein: 0.1g | Cholesterol: 10mg

INGREDIENTS

- 2 cups white sugar
- 1 cup butter
- 1 1/2 cups corn syrup
- 1 teaspoon vanilla extract
- 2 cups heavy cream

DIRECTIONS

1. Butter a 9x13 inch dish.
2. In a heavy saucepan, combine sugar, corn syrup, 1 cup cream and butter. Bring to a boil, stirring often, then stir in remaining 1 cup cream. Heat, without stirring, to 242 degrees F (116 degrees C), or until a small amount of syrup dropped into cold water forms a firm but pliable ball. Remove from heat, stir in vanilla, and pour into prepared dish. Refrigerate.
3. When cool, return candies to room temperature then cut into 1 inch squares and wrap in waxed paper.

GERMAN CHOCOLATE FUDGE
Servings: 8 | Prep: 15m | Cooks: 6m | Total: 2h21m

NUTRITION FACTS

Calories: 134 | Carbohydrates: 20.8g | Fat: 5.8g | Protein: 1.2g | Cholesterol: 2mg

INGREDIENTS

- 2 cups semisweet chocolate chips

- 2 tablespoons butter
- 12 (1 ounce) squares German sweet chocolate
- 1 (12 fluid ounce) can evaporated milk
- 1 (7 ounce) jar marshmallow creme
- 1/8 teaspoon salt
- 4 1/2 cups white sugar
- 2 cups chopped pecans

DIRECTIONS

1. Combine chocolate chips, German sweet chocolate and marshmallow creme in large bowl.
2. Combine sugar, butter, evaporated milk and salt in heavy skillet. Bring to a boil over medium heat. Cook for 6 minutes, stirring constantly.
3. Pour hot syrup over chocolate mixture. Stir with wooden spoon until smooth. Stir in pecans.
4. Spread into buttered 10x15 inch pan. Let stand until firm; cut into squares.

EMILY'S FAMOUS MARSHMALLOWS
Servings: 18 | Prep: 30m | Cooks: 20m | Total: 8h40m

NUTRITION FACTS

Calories: 118 | Carbohydrates: 29.8g | Fat: 0g | Protein: 0.4g | Cholesterol: 0mg

INGREDIENTS

- 1 cup confectioners' sugar for dusting
- 4 tablespoons unflavored gelatin
- 2 cups white sugar
- 2 egg whites
- 1 tablespoon light corn syrup
- 1 teaspoon vanilla extract
- 1 1/4 cups water, divided

DIRECTIONS

1. Dust a 9x9 inch square dish generously with confectioners' sugar.
2. In a small saucepan over medium-high heat, stir together white sugar, corn syrup and 3/4 cup water. Heat to 250 to 265 degrees F (121 to 129 degrees C), or until a small amount of syrup dropped into cold water forms a rigid ball.
3. While syrup is heating, place remaining water in a metal bowl and sprinkle gelatin over the surface. Place bowl over simmering water until gelatin has dissolved completely. Keep in a warm place until syrup has come to temperature. Remove syrup from heat and whisk gelatin mixture into hot syrup. Set aside.

4. In a separate bowl, whip egg whites to soft peaks. Continue to beat, pouring syrup mixture into egg whites in a thin stream, until the egg whites are very stiff. Stir in vanilla. Spread evenly in prepared pan and let rest 8 hours or overnight before cutting.

CARAMEL CORN
Servings: 8 | Prep: 20m | Cooks: 25m | Total: 45m

NUTRITION FACTS

Calories: 300 | Carbohydrates: 44.6g | Fat: 13.3g | Protein: 3.2g | Cholesterol: 23mg

INGREDIENTS

- 1 cup unpopped popcorn
- 3 tablespoons light corn syrup
- 2 tablespoons vegetable oil
- 1/4 teaspoon salt
- 3/4 cup packed brown sugar
- 1/4 teaspoon baking soda
- 6 tablespoons butter
- 1/4 teaspoon vanilla extract

DIRECTIONS

1. Preheat oven to 300 degrees F(150 degrees C).
2. In a large pot, heat oil over high heat. Add the unpopped popcorn. Moving the pan constantly, pop the corn. Remove from heat, place in a large baking pan, and keep warm in the preheated oven. Discard unpopped kernels.
3. Mix sugar, butter, corn syrup, and salt into a large saucepan. Cook over medium heat, stirring until mixture starts to boil. Continue cooking for 5 minutes without stirring.
4. Remove from heat. Stir in baking soda and vanilla. Pour over the popped popcorn. Stir popcorn until evenly coated. Bake for 25 to 30 minutes in the preheated oven, stirring every 10 minutes. Remove from pan and put into a large bowl to cool.

WHITE CHOCOLATE COVERED PRETZELS
Servings: 16 | Prep: 30m | Cooks: 10m | Total: 55m

NUTRITION FACTS

Calories: 77 | Carbohydrates: 8.9g | Fat: 4.3g | Protein: 0.9g | Cholesterol: 2mg

INGREDIENTS

- 6 (1 ounce) squares white chocolate
- 1 (15 ounce) package mini twist pretzels

- 1/4 cup red and green candy sprinkles (optional)

DIRECTIONS

1. Melt white chocolate in the top of a double boiler, stirring constantly.
2. Dip pretzel halfway into the white chocolate, completely covering half of the pretzel. Roll in topping if desired, and lay on wax paper.
3. Continue the process until all of the white chocolate is finished. Place in refrigerator for 15 minutes to harden. Store in airtight container.

BOARDWALK QUALITY MAPLE WALNUT FUDGE
Servings: 18 | Prep: 10m | Cooks: 5m | Total: 1h15m

NUTRITION FACTS

Calories: 328 | Carbohydrates: 30.2g | Fat: 21.5g | Protein: 5.4g | Cholesterol: 21mg

INGREDIENTS

- 3 cups white chocolate chips
- 1 teaspoon maple flavored extract
- 1 (14 ounce) can sweetened condensed milk
- 1 1/2 cups broken walnuts
- 1/4 cup butter

DIRECTIONS

1. Grease an 8x8-inch glass baking dish, and line with an 8x12-inch sheet of parchment paper. The ends will hang over the side of the dish.
2. Melt the white chocolate, sweetened condensed milk, and butter in a microwave-safe glass or ceramic bowl in 30-second intervals, stirring after each melting, for 1 to 3 minutes (depending on your microwave). Do not overheat or chocolate will scorch. Stir in the maple flavored extract until just combined, then add the walnuts. Pour chocolate mixture into the prepared baking dish; refrigerate until set, about 1 hour. Remove fudge by lifting the parchment paper, then cut into squares.

LAYERED MINT CHOCOLATE FUDGE
Servings: 30 | Prep: 20m | Cooks: 2h | Total: 2h20m

NUTRITION FACTS

Calories: 146 | Carbohydrates: 14.6g | Fat: 6.6g | Protein: 1.3g | Cholesterol: 6mg

INGREDIENTS

- 2 cups semi-sweet chocolate chips

- 6 ounces white confectioners coating* or premium white chocolate chips
- 1 (14 ounce) can EAGLE BRAND Sweetened Condensed Milk, divided
- 1 tablespoon peppermint extract
- 2 teaspoons vanilla extract
- Green or red food coloring (optional)

DIRECTIONS

1. In heavy saucepan, over low heat, melt chocolate chips with 1 cup sweetened condensed milk; add vanilla. Spread half the mixture into wax-paper-lined 8- or 9-inch square pan; chill 10 minutes or until firm. Hold remaining chocolate mixture at room temperature.
2. In heavy saucepan, over low heat, melt white confectioners coating with remaining sweetened condensed milk (mixture will be thick). Add peppermint extract and food coloring (optional).
3. Spread on chilled chocolate layer; chill 10 minutes longer or until firm.
4. Spread reserved chocolate mixture on mint layer. Chill 2 hours or until firm. Turn onto cutting board; peel off paper and cut into squares. Store leftovers covered in refrigerator.

CANDIED APPLES
Servings: 15 | Prep: 10m | Cooks: 30m | Total: 40m

NUTRITION FACTS

Calories: 237 | Carbohydrates: 62.5g | Fat: 0.2g | Protein: 0.4g | Cholesterol: 0mg

INGREDIENTS

- 15 apples
- 1 1/2 cups water
- 2 cups white sugar
- 8 drops red food coloring
- 1 cup light corn syrup

DIRECTIONS

1. Lightly grease cookie sheets. Insert craft sticks into whole, stemmed apples.
2. In a medium saucepan over medium-high heat, combine sugar, corn syrup and water. Heat to 300 to 310 degrees F (149 to 154 degrees C), or until a small amount of syrup dropped into cold water forms hard, brittle threads. Remove from heat and stir in food coloring.
3. Holding apple by its stick, dip in syrup and remove and turn to coat evenly. Place on prepared sheets to harden.

PEANUT BUTTER FUDGE
Servings: 16 | Prep: 5m | Cooks: 10m | Total: 45m

NUTRITION FACTS

Calories: 274 | Carbohydrates: 39.8g | Fat: 11.5g | Protein: 5.5g | Cholesterol: 7mg

INGREDIENTS

- 3/4 cup evaporated milk
- 1 1/8 cups peanut butter
- 2 cups sugar
- 2 cups marshmallow creme
- 2 tablespoons butter
- 1 teaspoon vanilla extract

DIRECTIONS

1. Grease an 8x8 inch dish.
2. In a medium saucepan over medium heat, combine milk, sugar and butter. Bring to a rolling boil, and let boil 5 minutes. Remove from heat and stir in peanut butter, marshmallow creme and vanilla until well incorporated. Spread into prepared dish. Let cool completely before cutting into squares.

CINNAMON-SUGAR POPCORN
Servings: 16 | Prep: 4m | Cooks: 40m | Total: 1h45m

NUTRITION FACTS

Calories: 114 | Carbohydrates: 17.8g | Fat: 4.4g | Protein: 1.6g | Cholesterol: 10mg

INGREDIENTS

- 1 cup unpopped popcorn
- 2 teaspoons ground cinnamon
- 1/3 cup butter
- 1/2 teaspoon salt
- 2/3 cup white sugar
- 1/2 teaspoon vanilla extract

DIRECTIONS

1. Preheat an oven to 250 degrees F (120 degrees C). Pop the popcorn using an air popper according to manufacturer's directions. Place into a large mixing bowl, and set aside.
2. Melt the butter in a small saucepan over medium heat. Stir in the sugar, cinnamon, salt, and vanilla, and cook until thick and bubbly. Pour over the popcorn, and stir until the popcorn is evenly coated. Spread the popcorn into a large roasting pan.
3. Bake in the preheated oven 10 minutes, then turn the heat off, and allow the popcorn to stay in the oven 20 minutes longer. Remove from oven, and cool completely before serving.

PEANUT BUTTER CANDY BARS

Servings: 35 | Prep: 20m | Cooks: 10m | Total: 30m

NUTRITION FACTS

Calories: 305 | Carbohydrates: 28.1g | Fat: 21.1g | Protein: 4.5g | Cholesterol: 0mg

INGREDIENTS

- 1 1/2 cups margarine, melted
- 2 cups graham cracker crumbs
- 2 cups peanut butter
- 1/2 cup margarine
- 4 1/2 cups confectioners' sugar
- 2 cups semisweet chocolate chips

DIRECTIONS

1. Grease a 10x15 inch pan. In a large bowl, combine 1 1/2 cups melted margarine, peanut butter, confectioners' sugar and graham cracker crumbs. Spread in prepared pan.
2. Combine 1/2 cup margarine and chocolate chips in a medium saucepan over medium-low heat. Stir occasionally until melted and smooth. Spread over peanut butter mixture. Let cool completely before cutting into bars.

CARAMEL PEANUT FUDGE

Servings: 96 | Prep: 30m | Cooks: 30m | Total: 2h20m

NUTRITION FACTS

Calories: 85 | Carbohydrates: 10.1g | Fat: 4.6g | Protein: 1.5g | Cholesterol: 4mg

INGREDIENTS

- 1 cup milk chocolate chips
- 1 teaspoon vanilla extract
- 1/4 cup butterscotch chips
- 1 1/2 cups chopped salted peanuts
- 1/4 cup creamy peanut butter
- 1 (14 ounce) package individually wrapped caramels, unwrapped
- 1/4 cup butter
- 1/4 cup heavy cream
- 1 cup white sugar
- 1 cup milk chocolate chips
- 1/4 cup evaporated milk

- 1/4 cup butterscotch chips
- 1 1/2 cups marshmallow creme
- 1/4 cup creamy peanut butter
- 1/4 cup creamy peanut butter

DIRECTIONS

1. Lightly grease a 9x13 inch dish.
2. For the bottom layer: Combine 1 cup milk chocolate chips, 1/4 cup butterscotch chips and 1/4 cup creamy peanut butter in a small saucepan over low heat. Cook and stir until melted and smooth. Spread evenly in prepared pan. Refrigerate until set.
3. For the filling: In a heavy saucepan over medium-high heat, melt butter. Stir in sugar and evaporated milk. Bring to a boil, and let boil 5 minutes. Remove from heat and stir in marshmallow creme, 1/4 cup peanut butter and vanilla. Fold in peanuts. Spread over bottom layer, return to refrigerator until set.
4. For the caramel: Combine caramels and cream in a medium saucepan over low heat. Cook and stir until melted and smooth. Spread over filling. Chill until set.
5. For the top layer: In a small saucepan over low heat, combine 1 cup milk chocolate chips, 1/4 cup butterscotch chips, and 1/4 cup peanut butter. Cook and stir until melted and smooth. Spread over caramel layer. Chill 1 hour before cutting into 1 inch squares.

KENTUCKY BOURBON BALLS
Servings: 24 | Prep: 20m | Cooks: 10m | Total: 16h30m

NUTRITION FACTS

Calories: 252 | Carbohydrates: 31.3g | Fat: 13.9g | Protein: 2.3g | Cholesterol: 10mg

INGREDIENTS

- 1 cup chopped nuts
- 1 (16 ounce) package confectioners' sugar
- 5 tablespoons Kentucky bourbon
- 18 ounces semisweet chocolate
- 1/2 cup butter, softened

DIRECTIONS

1. Place the nuts in a sealable jar. Pour the bourbon over the nuts. Seal and allow to soak overnight.
2. Mix the butter and sugar; fold in the soaked nuts. Form into 3/4" balls and refrigerate overnight.
3. Line a tray with waxed paper. Melt the chocolate in the top of a double boiler over just-barely simmering water, stirring frequently and scraping down the sides with a rubber spatula to avoid scorching. Roll the balls in the melted chocolate to coat; arrange on the prepared tray. Store in refrigerator until serving.

SPOOKY HALLOWEEN EYEBALLS

Servings: 30 | Prep: 20m | Cooks: 3h | Total: 3h20m

NUTRITION FACTS

Calories: 227 | Carbohydrates: 21.4g | Fat: 14.9g | Protein: 4g | Cholesterol: 10mg

INGREDIENTS

- 1 1/2 cups creamy peanut butter
- 2 tablespoons shortening
- 1/2 cup butter, softened
- 2 drops blue food coloring
- 2 1/2 cups confectioners' sugar, sifted
- 1/2 cup miniature semisweet chocolate chips
- 1 tablespoon vanilla extract
- red food coloring (optional)
- 12 ounces white chocolate, chopped

DIRECTIONS

1. Beat the peanut butter and butter with an electric mixer in a large bowl until smooth. Beat in the sugar and vanilla. Cover and refrigerate for 30 minutes. Roll chilled dough into small, eyeball-sized balls and place on 2 baking sheets lined with wax paper. Refrigerate for another 30 minutes.
2. Melt the white chocolate and shortening in a microwave-safe glass or ceramic bowl in 30-second intervals, stirring after each melting, for 1 to 3 minutes (depending on your microwave). Do not overheat or chocolate will scorch. Dip each eyeball into the white chocolate and transfer to the waxed paper until the chocolate has set. You can chill them in the refrigerator.
3. Stir a few drops of blue food coloring into the remaining melted white chocolate. Make a round "iris" on the top of the cooled eyeball and press a mini chocolate chip in the center for a "pupil." For an extra spooky bloodshot eyeballs take a toothpick dipped in red food coloring and make squiggly lines on the eye.

ALMOND CRUNCH

Servings: 16 | Prep: 15m | Cooks: 30m | Total: 2h20m

NUTRITION FACTS

Calories: 317 | Carbohydrates: 32.6g | Fat: 21g | Protein: 3g | Cholesterol: 35mg

INGREDIENTS

- 1 cup blanched slivered almonds
- 2 tablespoons light corn syrup
- 1 cup butter

- 2 tablespoons water
- 1 1/4 cups white sugar
- 2 cups milk chocolate chips

DIRECTIONS

1. Preheat oven to 375 degrees F (190 degrees C). Arrange almonds in a single layer on a baking sheet. Toast in the preheated oven until lightly browned, approximately 5 minutes.
2. Line a jelly roll pan with foil.
3. In a heavy saucepan, combine butter, sugar, corn syrup, and water. Cook over medium heat, stirring constantly, until mixture boils. Boil, without stirring, to hard crack stage, 300 degrees F (150 degrees C). Remove from heat.
4. Working quickly, stir in almonds, and pour mixture into foil lined jelly roll pan; tip pan from side to side to spread candy evenly in pan. Sprinkle chocolate chips over candy brittle. Let stand about 5 minutes, or until shiny and soft. Spread chocolate evenly over candy. Cool to room temperature, then refrigerate for 1 hour. Break into bite-size pieces.

RASPBERRY TRUFFLE FUDGE

Servings: 40 | Prep: 10m | Cooks: 10m | Total: 1h20m

NUTRITION FACTS

Calories: 149 | Carbohydrates: 19.7g | Fat: 7.5g | Protein: 2.3g | Cholesterol: 5mg

INGREDIENTS

- 3 cups semi-sweet chocolate chips
- 1/4 cup heavy cream
- 1 (14 ounce) can sweetened condensed milk
- 1/4 cup raspberry flavored liqueur
- 1 1/2 teaspoons vanilla extract
- 2 cups semi-sweet chocolate chips
- salt to taste

DIRECTIONS

1. Spray a 9x9 inch pan with non-stick cooking spray, and line with wax paper.
2. In a microwave-safe bowl, combine 3 cups chocolate chips and sweetened condensed milk. Heat in microwave until chocolate melts, stirring occasionally. Be careful not to let it scorch. Stir in the vanilla and salt. Spread into pan, and cool to room temperature.
3. In a microwave-safe bowl, combine cream, liqueur, and 2 cups chocolate chips. Heat in microwave until the chocolate melts; stir until smooth. Cool to lukewarm, then pour over the fudge layer. Refrigerate until both layers are completely set, about 1 hour. Cut into 1 inch pieces.

LAYERED PEPPERMINT BARK
Servings: 32 | Prep: 30m | Cooks: 55m | Total: 1h25m

NUTRITION FACTS

Calories: 204 | Carbohydrates: 28.7g | Fat: 9.5g | Protein: 1.6g | Cholesterol: 8mg

INGREDIENTS

- 20 ounces white chocolate, coarsely chopped, divided
- 6 tablespoons heavy cream
- 30 peppermint candies, crushed, divided
- 1 teaspoon peppermint extract
- 10 ounces dark chocolate, coarsely chopped

DIRECTIONS

1. Line a 9x12 inch baking pan with aluminum foil or parchment paper.
2. Melt half of the white chocolate in the top of a double boiler over just barely simmering water, stirring frequently and scraping down the sides with a rubber spatula to avoid scorching. Spread the white chocolate into the prepared pan. Sprinkle 1/4 of the crushed peppermints evenly over white chocolate. Chill until firm, about 15 minutes.
3. Meanwhile, melt the dark chocolate, heavy cream, and peppermint extract together in the top of a double boiler over just barely simmering water, stirring frequently, until just melted. Quickly pour the chocolate layer over the chilled white chocolate layer; spread evenly. Chill until firm, about 20 minutes.
4. Meanwhile, melt the remaining white chocolate in the top of a double boiler over just barely simmering water, stirring frequently, until just melted. Spread quickly over the chilled bark. Sprinkle with the remaining peppermint pieces; chill until firm, about 20 minutes. Cut or break into small pieces to serve.

HARD ROCK CANDY
Servings: 48 | Prep: 15m | Cooks: 45m | Total: 2h

NUTRITION FACTS

Calories: 100 | Carbohydrates: 26.1g | Fat: 0g | Protein: 0g | Cholesterol: 0mg

INGREDIENTS

- 1 cup confectioners' sugar
- 1 cup water
- 3 3/4 cups white sugar
- 2 teaspoons cinnamon oil
- 1 1/2 cups light corn syrup
- 1 teaspoon red food coloring

DIRECTIONS

1. Roll the edges of two 16 inch square pieces of heavy duty aluminum foil. Sprinkle the foil very generously with confectioners' sugar.
2. In a large heavy saucepan, combine the white sugar, corn syrup, and water. Heat over medium-high heat, stirring constantly until sugar dissolves. Stop stirring, and boil until a candy thermometer reads 300 to 310 degrees F (149 to 154 degrees C). Remove from heat.
3. Stir in the cinnamon oil and food coloring. Pour onto the prepared foil, and allow to cool and harden. Crack into pieces, and store in an airtight container.

QUEIJADAS
Servings: 18 | Prep: 10m | Cooks: 45m | Total: 55m

NUTRITION FACTS

Calories: 148 | Carbohydrates: 27.5g | Fat: 3.3g | Protein: 2.5g | Cholesterol: 38mg

INGREDIENTS

- 3 eggs
- 3/4 cup all-purpose flour
- 2 cups white sugar
- 2 cups milk
- 3 tablespoons butter
- 1/2 teaspoon vanilla extract

DIRECTIONS

1. Preheat oven to 325 degrees F (165 degrees C).
2. In a blender, combine eggs, sugar and butter. Blend until smooth. Pour in flour and milk, a little at a time, blending until smooth again. Stir in vanilla.
3. Pour into muffin tins, filling 3/4 full. Bake in preheated oven 45 minutes, until golden brown. Serve hot or cold.

SODA CRACKER CANDY
Servings: 8 | Prep: 10m | Cooks: 10m | Total: 20m

NUTRITION FACTS

Calories: 1151 | Carbohydrates: 123g | Fat: 75.7g | Protein: 12.2g | Cholesterol: 92mg

INGREDIENTS

- 1 (10 ounce) package saltine crackers
- 2 (12 ounce) packages semisweet chocolate chips

- 1 1/2 cups butter
- 2 cups chopped almonds
- 1 1/2 cups packed brown sugar

DIRECTIONS

1. Preheat oven to 400 degrees F (200 degrees C). Line a 10x15 inch cookie sheet with aluminum foil.
2. Place crackers in a singe layer over prepared cookie sheet. Use more or fewer crackers as needed to cover the bottom of your pan.
3. In a small saucepan over low heat combine butter and brown sugar; bring to a boil. Boil for 3 minutes; pour over crackers.
4. Bake in preheated oven for 5 minutes. Sprinkle chocolate chips evenly over the top. Sprinkle almonds over chocolate chips; using the back of a wooden spoon, press nuts into chocolate.
5. Chill in refrigerator for at least 3 hours, or until set. Break into pieces and store, sealed, in refrigerator.

ROCKY ROAD CANDIES
Servings: 24 | Prep: 5m | Cooks: 5m | Total: 2h10m

NUTRITION FACTS

Calories: 284 | Carbohydrates: 36.3g | Fat: 14.1g | Protein: 5.5g | Cholesterol: 8mg

INGREDIENTS

- 1 (12 ounce) package semisweet chocolate chips
- 2 1/2 cups dry-roasted peanuts
- 1/8 cup butter
- 1 (16 ounce) package miniature marshmallows
- 1 (14 ounce) can sweetened condensed milk

DIRECTIONS

1. Line a 9 x 13 inch pan with wax paper.
2. In a microwave-safe bowl, microwave chocolate and butter until melted. Stir occasionally until chocolate is smooth. Stir in condensed milk. Combine peanuts and marshmallows; stir into chocolate mixture. Pour into prepared pan and chill until firm. Cut into squares.

BASIC TRUFFLES
Servings: 35 | Prep: 10m | Cooks: 10m | Total: 1h50m

NUTRITION FACTS

Calories: 62 | Carbohydrates: 5.6g | Fat: 4.1g | Protein: 0.7g | Cholesterol: 4mg

INGREDIENTS

- 12 ounces bittersweet chocolate, chopped
- 1/3 cup heavy cream
- 1 teaspoon vanilla extract

DIRECTIONS

1. In a medium saucepan over medium heat, combine chocolate and cream. Cook, stirring, until chocolate is melted and mixture is smooth. Remove from heat and whisk in flavoring. Pour into a small dish and refrigerate until set, but not hard, 1 1/2 to 2 hours. Use to fill candies or form balls and roll in toppings.

WHITE CHOCOLATE FUDGE
Servings: 40 | Prep: 15m | Cooks: 10m | Total: 1h25m

NUTRITION FACTS

Calories: 126 | Carbohydrates: 17.4g | Fat: 6.1g | Protein: 1.1g | Cholesterol: 8mg

INGREDIENTS

- 1 (8 ounce) package cream cheese
- 12 ounces white chocolate, chopped
- 4 cups confectioners' sugar
- 3/4 cup chopped pecans
- 1 1/2 teaspoons vanilla extract

DIRECTIONS

1. Grease an 8x8 inch baking dish. Set aside.
2. In a medium bowl, beat cream cheese, sugar, and vanilla until smooth.
3. In the top of a double boiler over lightly simmering water, heat white chocolate, stirring until melted and smooth.
4. Fold melted white chocolate and pecans into cream cheese mixture. Spread into prepared baking dish. Chill for 1 hour, then cut into 1 inch squares.

ORANGE CREAM FUDGE
Servings: 24 | Prep: 15m | Cooks: 5m | Total: 2h20m

NUTRITION FACTS

Calories: 271 | Carbohydrates: 38.9g | Fat: 12.8g | Protein: 1.2g | Cholesterol: 27mg

INGREDIENTS

- 3 cups white sugar
- 1 (11 ounce) package white chocolate chips
- 2/3 cup heavy cream
- 3 teaspoons orange extract
- 3/4 cup butter
- 12 drops yellow food coloring
- 1 (7 ounce) jar marshmallow creme
- 9 drops red food coloring

DIRECTIONS

1. Grease a 9 x 13 inch pan.
2. In a medium saucepan over medium heat, combine sugar, cream and butter. Heat to soft ball stage, 234 degrees F (112 degrees C). Remove from heat and stir in marshmallow creme and white chocolate chips; mix well until the chips melt. Reserve 1 cup of mixture and set aside.
3. To the remaining mixture add orange flavoring, yellow and red food coloring. Stir well and pour into prepared pan. Pour reserved cream mixture on top. Using a knife, swirl layers for decorative effect.
4. Chill for 2 hours, or until firm, and cut into squares.

EASTER EGGS
Servings: 60 | Prep: 3h | Cooks: 10m | Total: 3h10m

NUTRITION FACTS

Calories: 226 | Carbohydrates: 25.2g | Fat: 14.3g | Protein: 2.7g | Cholesterol: 4mg

INGREDIENTS

- 2 pounds confectioners' sugar
- 12 ounces peanut butter
- 1/4 pound margarine, softened
- 1 pound flaked coconut
- 1 (8 ounce) package cream cheese
- 4 cups semisweet chocolate chips
- 2 teaspoons vanilla extract
- 2 tablespoons shortening

DIRECTIONS

1. In a mixing bowl, combine sugar, margarine, cream cheese and vanilla extract. Divide the batter in half and place each half of the batter in a bowl on its own. Stir peanut butter into one of the bowls and coconut into the second.
2. Using your hands, mold the dough into egg-shapes and arrange the forms on cookie sheets. Place the eggs in the freezer until frozen.

3. Once the eggs have frozen, melt the chocolate and shortening in the top of a double-boiler. Dip the eggs into the chocolate until coated. Place the eggs on wax paper lined cookie sheets and return to the freezer to harden. After the chocolate has hardened the eggs can be kept in the refrigerator.

FROSTED CRANBERRIES
Servings: 24 | Prep: 5m | Cooks: 2h | Total: 2h5m

NUTRITION FACTS

Calories: 39 | Carbohydrates: 10g | Fat: 0g | Protein: 0.1g | Cholesterol: <1mg

INGREDIENTS

- 2 tablespoons water
- 1 (12 ounce) package fresh cranberries
- 1 tablespoon pasteurized egg white or liquid egg substitute
- 1 cup white sugar

DIRECTIONS

1. In a medium bowl, stir together the water and egg white until blended but not whipped. Coat cranberries with this mixture. Spread the sugar out on a baking sheet, and roll the cranberries in it until they are coated. Dry at room temperature for 2 hours. Use as garnishes for desserts, or eat them plain.

MAGIC WANDS
Servings: 30 | Prep: 30m | Cooks: 0m | Total: 30m

NUTRITION FACTS

Calories: 134 | Carbohydrates: 23.7g | Fat: 3.6g | Protein: 1.6g | Cholesterol: <1mg

INGREDIENTS

- 1 (15 ounce) package pretzel rods
- 1 (16 ounce) container prepared vanilla frosting
- 1/2 cup sprinkles or colored sugar for decoration

DIRECTIONS

1. Dip each pretzel rod into frosting, not quite half way. Roll in sprinkles to coat the frosting. Abracadabra, you have a magic wand.

CHOCOLATE COVERED CARAMELS

Servings: 120 | Prep: 5m | Cooks: 25m | Total: 2h25m

NUTRITION FACTS

Calories: 63 | Carbohydrates: 8.8g | Fat: 3g | Protein: 0.6g | Cholesterol: 6mg

INGREDIENTS

- 1 cup butter
- 1 teaspoon vanilla extract
- 2 1/4 cups brown sugar
- 1 pound milk chocolate
- 1 cup light corn syrup
- 1 tablespoon butter
- 1 (14 ounce) can sweetened condensed milk

DIRECTIONS

1. Grease an 8 x 8 inch square pan.
2. In a heavy 4 quart saucepan melt butter over medium heat; add brown sugar, corn syrup and milk. Stirring constantly, heat to 242 to 248 degrees F (116 to 120 degrees C), or until a small amount of syrup dropped into cold water forms a firm but pliable ball. Remove from heat and stir in vanilla extract. Pour into prepared pan.
3. When caramel has cooled and set, cut into 1 inch squares. Chill in refrigerator until firm.
4. Melt chocolate with 1 tablespoon butter in the top of a double boiler or in a bowl in the microwave. Stir until smooth.
5. Dip caramel squares in chocolate and place on wax paper to cool.

ANGEL FOOD CANDY

Servings: 30 | Prep: 20m | Cooks: 30m | Total: 1h15m

NUTRITION FACTS

Calories: 129 | Carbohydrates: 22.2g | Fat: 6g | Protein: 1.2g | Cholesterol: 0mg

INGREDIENTS

- 1 cup white sugar
- 1 tablespoon baking soda
- 1 cup dark corn syrup
- 1 pound chocolate confectioners' coating
- 1 tablespoon vinegar

DIRECTIONS

1. Butter a 9x13 inch baking dish.
2. In a medium saucepan over medium heat, combine sugar, corn syrup and vinegar. Cook, stirring, until sugar dissolves. Heat, without stirring, to 300 to 310 degrees F (149 to 154 degrees C), or until a small amount of syrup dropped into cold water forms hard, brittle threads.
3. Remove from heat and stir in baking soda. Pour into prepared pan; do not spread. (Mixture will not fill pan.) Allow to cool completely.
4. In the microwave or over a double boiler, melt coating chocolate, stirring frequently until smooth. Break cooled candy into bite-sized pieces and dip into melted candy coating. Let set on waxed paper. Store tightly covered.

CHOCOLATE WALNUT FUDGE
Servings: 36 | Prep: 10m | Cooks: 15m | Total: 2h

NUTRITION FACTS

Calories: 121 | Carbohydrates: 16.5g | Fat: 6.4g | Protein: 1g | Cholesterol: 8mg

INGREDIENTS

- 1/2 cup butter
- 5 ounces evaporated milk
- 1 cup semisweet chocolate chips
- 10 large marshmallows
- 1 teaspoon vanilla extract
- 1 cup chopped walnuts
- 2 cups white sugar

DIRECTIONS

1. Butter an 8x8 inch dish.
2. Place butter, chocolate chips and vanilla in a mixing bowl. Set aside.
3. In a medium saucepan over medium heat, combine sugar, milk and marshmallows. Bring to a boil, stirring frequently. Reduce heat to low and cook 6 minutes more, stirring constantly. Remove from heat.
4. Pour marshmallow mixture over contents of mixing bowl. Beat entire mixture until it thickens and loses its gloss. Quickly fold in nuts and pour into prepared pan. Refrigerate several hours until firm.

EAGLE BRAND PEANUT BUTTER FUDGE
Servings: 64 | Prep: 20m | Cooks: 2h | Total: 2h20m

NUTRITION FACTS

Calories: 79 | Carbohydrates: 5.9g | Fat: 4.2g | Protein: 1.5g | Cholesterol: 3mg

INGREDIENTS

- 1 (14 ounce) can EAGLE BRAND Sweetened Condensed Milk
- 3/4 cup chopped peanuts
- 1/2 cup Jif Creamy Peanut Butter
- 1 teaspoon vanilla extract
- 2 (6 ounce) packages white chocolate squares or white baking bars, chopped

DIRECTIONS

1. In heavy saucepan, heat sweetened condensed milk and peanut butter over medium heat until just bubbly, stirring constantly. Remove from heat. Stir in white chocolate until smooth. Immediately stir in peanuts and vanilla.
2. Spread evenly into wax paper lined 8-or 9-inch square pan. Cool. Cover and chill 2 hours or until firm. Turn fudge onto cutting board; peel off paper. Sprinkle with additional chopped peanuts if desired. Cut into squares. Store leftovers covered in refrigerator.

GRANDMA'S PEANUT BUTTER FUDGE
Servings: 24 | Prep: 20m | Cooks: 40m | Total: 1h

NUTRITION FACTS

Calories: 308 | Carbohydrates: 43.7g | Fat: 14.3g | Protein: 3.8g | Cholesterol: 25mg

INGREDIENTS

- 4 cups white sugar
- 1 cup crunchy peanut butter
- 1 (12 fluid ounce) can evaporated milk
- 1 (7 ounce) jar marshmallow creme
- 1 cup butter

DIRECTIONS

1. Butter a 9x13 inch baking dish and set aside. Butter a 3 quart saucepan.
2. Place buttered saucepan over medium heat, and combine sugar, evaporated milk and 1 cup butter within. Heat to between 234 and 240 degrees F (112 to 116 degrees C), or until a small amount of syrup dropped into cold water forms a soft ball that flattens when removed from the water and placed on a flat surface.
3. Remove from heat and stir in peanut butter and marshmallow creme. Beat vigorously until smooth. Pour quickly into prepared baking dish. Let cool completely before cutting into squares.

EASY TOFFEE
Servings: 25 | Prep: 15m | Cooks: 15m | Total: 30m

NUTRITION FACTS

Calories: 236 | Carbohydrates: 25.9g | Fat: 14.9g | Protein: 2.6g | Cholesterol: 20mg

INGREDIENTS

- 1 (10 ounce) package saltine crackers
- 1 (12 ounce) package semisweet chocolate chips
- 1 cup butter
- 1 cup slivered almonds
- 1 cup light brown sugar

DIRECTIONS

1. Preheat oven to 325 degrees F (165 degrees C). Grease a baking sheet. Line baking sheet with saltine crackers, edges touching.
2. In a medium saucepan, combine butter and brown sugar and cook until mixture reaches 235 degrees F (112 degrees C) or a small amount of mixture dropped into cold water forms a small ball that flattens when placed on a flat surface. Pour mixture over crackers and spread evenly.
3. Bake in preheated oven 15 minutes. Sprinkle chocolate chips over hot toffee. When chips turn glossy, spread evenly with spatula. Sprinkle with almonds. Freeze 20 minutes before serving.

PURE MAPLE CANDY
Servings: 18 | Prep: 1m | Cooks: 10m | Total: 51m

NUTRITION FACTS

Calories: 113 | Carbohydrates: 23.9g | Fat: 2.2g | Protein: 0.5g | Cholesterol: 0mg

INGREDIENTS

- 2 cups pure maple syrup
- 1/2 cup chopped walnuts (optional)

DIRECTIONS

1. In a large heavy-bottomed saucepan, bring the maple syrup to a boil over medium-high heat stirring occasionally. Boil until syrup reaches 235 degrees F (110 degrees C) on a candy thermometer.
2. Remove from heat and cool to 175 degrees F (80 degrees C) without stirring, about 10 minutes.
3. Stir mixture rapidly with a wooden spoon for about 5 minutes until the color turns lighter and mixture becomes thick and creamy. Stir in chopped nuts, if desired.
4. Pour into molds. Set aside to cool. Once cool, unmold candy. Store in airtight containers up to 1 month.

CHOCOLATE COVERED EASTER EGGS
Servings: 48 | Prep: 30m | Cooks: 2h | Total: 2h30m

NUTRITION FACTS

Calories: 204 | Carbohydrates: 30.9g | Fat: 9.3g | Protein: 2.4g | Cholesterol: 10mg

INGREDIENTS

- 1/2 cup butter, softened
- 1 cup flaked coconut (optional)
- 1 teaspoon vanilla extract
- 1 cup unsweetened cocoa powder (optional)
- 1 (8 ounce) package cream cheese, softened
- 2 cups semisweet chocolate pieces
- 2 1/2 pounds confectioners' sugar
- 1 tablespoon shortening or vegetable oil (optional)
- 1 cup creamy peanut butter (optional)

DIRECTIONS

1. In a large bowl, mix together the butter, vanilla, and cream cheese. Stir in confectioners' sugar to make a workable dough. For best results, use your hands for mixing.
2. Divide the dough into four parts. Leave one of the parts plain. To the second part, mix in peanut butter. Mix coconut into the third part, and cocoa powder into the last part. Roll each type of dough into egg shapes, and place on a waxed paper-lined cookie sheet. Refrigerate until hard, at least an hour.
3. Melt chocolate chips in a heat-proof bowl over a pan of simmering water. Stir occasionally until smooth. If the chocolate seems too thick for coating, stir in a teaspoon of the shortening or oil until it thins to your desired consistency. Dip the chilled candy eggs in chocolate, and return to the waxed paper lined sheet to set. Refrigerate for 1/2 hour to harden.

OLD-FASHIONED DIVINITY CANDY
Servings: 18 | Prep: 20m | Cooks: 30m | Total: 50m

NUTRITION FACTS

Calories: 114 | Carbohydrates: 29.3g | Fat: 0g | Protein: 0.4g | Cholesterol: 0mg

INGREDIENTS

- 2 cups white sugar
- 1/4 teaspoon salt
- 1/2 cup light corn syrup
- 2 egg whites
- 1/2 cup hot water
- 1 teaspoon vanilla extract

DIRECTIONS

1. In a heavy, 2 quart saucepan, combine the sugar, corn syrup, hot water, and salt. Cook and stir until the sugar dissolves and the mixture comes to a boil. Then cook to hard ball stage without stirring, 250 degrees F (120 degrees C.) Frequently wipe crystals forming on the sides of the pan, using a pastry brush dipped in water. Remove from heat.
2. Just as the syrup is reaching temperature, begin whipping egg whites: In a large glass or stainless steel mixing bowl, beat egg whites until stiff peaks form. Pour hot syrup in a thin stream over beaten egg whites, beating constantly with the electric mixer at medium speed. Increase speed to high, and continue beating for about 5 minutes. Add vanilla; continue beating until the mixture becomes stiff and begins to lose its gloss. If it is too stiff, add a few drops hot water.
3. Immediately drop by teaspoonfuls onto waxed paper. For a decorative flair, twirl the top with the spoon when dropping. Let stand until set. Store in an airtight container at room temperature.

ACORN CANDY COOKIES
Servings: 24 | Prep: 15m | Cooks: 30m | Total: 45m

NUTRITION FACTS

Calories: 132 | Carbohydrates: 15.6g | Fat: 6.7g | Protein: 0.5g | Cholesterol: 1mg

INGREDIENTS

- 1 tablespoon prepared chocolate frosting
- 24 mini vanilla wafer cookies (such as Nilla)
- 24 milk chocolate candy kisses (such as Hershey's Kisses), unwrapped
- 24 butterscotch chips

DIRECTIONS

1. Smear a small amount of frosting onto the flat bottom of a candy kiss. Press onto the flat bottom of the vanilla wafer. Smear a little more frosting onto the flat bottom of a butterscotch chip, and press onto the rounded top of the cookie. Repeat with remaining ingredients. Set aside to dry, about 30 minutes.

EASY MICROWAVE PEANUT BRITTLE
Servings: 6 | Prep: 10m | Cooks: 8m | Total: 18m

NUTRITION FACTS

Calories: 439 | Carbohydrates: 62.3g | Fat: 20.1g | Protein: 8.7g | Cholesterol: 5mg

INGREDIENTS

- cooking spray

- 1 tablespoon butter
- 1 cup white sugar
- 1 teaspoon baking soda
- 1/2 cup light corn syrup
- 1 teaspoon vanilla extract
- 1 1/2 cups peanuts, or more to taste

DIRECTIONS

1. Spray a baking sheet and a wooden spoon with cooking spray.
2. Mix sugar and corn syrup together in a microwaveable bowl safe for high temperatures.
3. Heat sugar mixture in microwave on high for 5 minutes.
4. Stir peanuts and butter into sugar mixture. Heat in microwave until mixture becomes a caramel color, 3 to 4 minutes.
5. Mix baking soda and vanilla extract into syrup until smooth and foam has dissipated. Spread candy onto the prepared baking sheet using the sprayed wooden spoon. Work quickly; candy hardens fast. Let stand until cool. Break into pieces to serve.

JELLY BEAN NESTS
Servings: 12 | Prep: 25m | Cooks: 5m | Total: 30m

NUTRITION FACTS

Calories: 143 | Carbohydrates: 15.5g | Fat: 8.4g | Protein: 1.3g | Cholesterol: 10mg

INGREDIENTS

- 2 cups miniature marshmallows
- 1/4 cup butter
- 4 cups chow mein noodles

DIRECTIONS

1. Butter a 12 cup muffin tin
2. Combine marshmallows and butter over medium heat in a saucepan; stir until the butter and marshmallows have melted. Stir in the chow mein noodles, coat well. Butter fingers and press the mixture into the bottom and sides of the prepared muffin tin. Refrigerate until firm

CHOCOLATE COVERED PEPPERMINT PATTIES
Servings: 48 | Prep: 45m | Cooks: 5m | Total: 8h50m

NUTRITION FACTS

Calories: 118 | Carbohydrates: 24.3g | Fat: 2.6g | Protein: 0.4g | Cholesterol: 1mg

INGREDIENTS

- 1 cup mashed potatoes
- 8 cups confectioners' sugar
- 1 teaspoon salt
- 8 (1 ounce) squares semisweet chocolate
- 2 tablespoons melted butter
- 2 tablespoons shortening
- 2 teaspoons peppermint extract

DIRECTIONS

1. In a large bowl, mix together the potatoes, salt, butter, and peppermint extract. Gradually mix in confectioners' sugar; mix in enough to make a workable dough, between 6 and 8 cups.
2. Knead slightly, and roll into cherry-size balls. Flatten balls to form patties. Arrange on sheets of wax paper, and allow to dry overnight.
3. Place chocolate and shortening in a microwave-safe bowl. Heat in microwave, stirring occasionally, until melted and smooth. Dip patties in melted chocolate, and let cool on wax paper.

GOURMET CARAMEL APPLES

Servings: 5 | Prep: 5m | Cooks: 45m | Total: 50m

NUTRITION FACTS

Calories: 831 | Carbohydrates: 131.8g | Fat: 34.8g | Protein: 8.1g | Cholesterol: 22mg

INGREDIENTS

- 5 large Granny Smith apples
- 7 ounces chocolate candy bar, broken into pieces
- 1 (14 ounce) package individually wrapped caramels, unwrapped
- 2 tablespoons shortening, divided
- 2 tablespoons water
- 1 cup colored candy coating melts

DIRECTIONS

1. Bring a large pot of water to a boil. Dip apples into boiling water briefly, using a slotted spoon, to remove any wax that may be present. Wipe dry, and set aside to cool. Insert sticks into the apples through the cores.
2. Line a baking sheet with waxed paper and coat with cooking spray. Place the unwrapped caramels into a microwave-safe medium bowl along with 2 tablespoons of water. Cook on high for 2 minutes, then stir and continue cooking and stirring at 1 minute intervals until caramel is melted and smooth.
3. Hold apples by the stick, and dip into the caramel to coat. Set on waxed paper; refrigerate for about 15 minutes to set.

4. Heat the chocolate with 1 tablespoon of shortening in a microwave-safe bowl until melted and smooth. Dip apples into the chocolate to cover the layer of caramel. Return to the waxed paper to set.
5. Melt the candy melts in the microwave with the remaining shortening, stirring every 30 seconds until smooth. Use a fork or wooden stick to flick colored designs onto your apples for a finishing touch. Refrigerate until set, overnight is even better.

CHOCOLATE POPCORN
Servings: 16 | Prep: 10m | Cooks: 35m | Total: 1h45m

NUTRITION FACTS

Calories: 185 | Carbohydrates: 18.9g | Fat: 12g | Protein: 3g | Cholesterol: 15mg

INGREDIENTS

- 2 quarts popped popcorn
- 1/4 cup cocoa powder
- 1 cup peanuts (optional)
- 1/2 cup butter
- 3/4 cup sugar
- 1 teaspoon vanilla
- 1/4 cup corn syrup

DIRECTIONS

1. Preheat oven to 250 degrees F (120 degrees C). Oil a 10x15 inch baking pan with sides.
2. Place popcorn and peanuts into a large, metal bowl, and set aside. Stir together the sugar, corn syrup, cocoa powder, and butter in a saucepan over medium-high heat until it comes to a boil. Boil for 2 minutes. Stir in the vanilla, then pour over the popcorn. Stir until the popcorn is well coated. Spread the popcorn into the prepared pan.
3. Bake in preheated oven for 30 minutes, stirring several times.
4. Remove from the oven, and allow to cool to room temperature. Break into small clumps, and store in an airtight container.

CRISPY RICE CANDY
Servings: 84 | Prep: 15m | Cooks: 2h | Total: 2h15m

NUTRITION FACTS

Calories: 103 | Carbohydrates: 9.4g | Fat: 6.7g | Protein: 2.2g | Cholesterol: 2mg

INGREDIENTS

- 2 cups crispy rice cereal

- 1 cup crunchy peanut butter
- 2 cups dry roasted peanuts
- 2 pounds white chocolate, chopped
- 2 cups miniature marshmallows

DIRECTIONS

1. In a large bowl, combine cereal, peanuts, marshmallows and peanut butter. Stir until evenly mixed.
2. In a microwave-safe bowl, or in a double boiler, cook chocolate until melted. Stir occasionally until chocolate is smooth. Stir chocolate into cereal mixture. Mixture will be slightly runny.
3. Drop by tablespoons onto waxed paper. Let set until firm, 2 hours. Store in an airtight container.

PEANUT CLUSTERS
Servings: 6 | Prep: 10m | Cooks: 5m | Total: 20m

NUTRITION FACTS

Calories: 150 | Carbohydrates: 11.8g | Fat: 9.8g | Protein: 5g | Cholesterol: 0mg

INGREDIENTS

- 1 (12 ounce) package semi-sweet chocolate chips
- 1 (12 ounce) package peanut butter chips
- 12 ounces raw Spanish peanuts

DIRECTIONS

1. Combine chocolate chips and peanut butter chips in top of double boiler. Stir frequently over low to medium heat until melted; add peanuts and stir.
2. Drop by teaspoon full on wax paper. Allow to cool.

HALLOWEEN POPCORN PUMPKINS
Servings: 12 | Prep: 5m | Cooks: 5m | Total: 20m

NUTRITION FACTS

Calories: 328 | Carbohydrates: 45.4g | Fat: 15g | Protein: 3.8g | Cholesterol: 20mg

INGREDIENTS

- 5 cups popped popcorn
- 3 cups miniature marshmallows
- 1 cup candy corn
- 4 drops red food coloring

- 1 cup chopped salted peanuts
- 3 drops yellow food coloring
- 1/2 cup butter or margarine
- 4 sticks red or black licorice, cut into thirds

DIRECTIONS

1. Grease a muffin pan and set aside. Place popcorn, candy corn and peanuts into a large bowl and set aside.
2. Melt the butter in a large saucepan over medium heat. Stir in marshmallows, red food coloring and yellow food coloring, adjusting color if needed to get a nice shade of orange. When the marshmallows are completely melted, pour over the popcorn and stir to evenly distribute the candy, nuts and marshmallow.
3. Use a greased spoon to fill the muffin cups. Insert a piece of licorice to act as the stem, and mold the popcorn around it. Let stand until firm, 10 to 15 minutes, and then pull the pumpkins out by their stems and admire your pumpkin patch.

WORLD'S BEST OREO FUDGE
Servings: 48 | Prep: 15m | Cooks: 5m | Total: 20m

NUTRITION FACTS

Calories: 146 | Carbohydrates: 22.1g | Fat: 6.3g | Protein: 1g | Cholesterol: 10mg

INGREDIENTS

- 3 cups white sugar
- 1 (7 ounce) jar marshmallow creme
- 3/4 cup butter
- 1 teaspoon vanilla extract
- 2/3 cup evaporated milk
- 1/2 cup crumbled chocolate sandwich cookies (such as Oreo)
- 2 cups white chocolate chips
- 1 cup crushed chocolate sandwich cookies (such as Oreo)

DIRECTIONS

1. Line a 13x9-inch baking pan with parchment paper.
2. Bring sugar, butter, and evaporated milk to a boil in a heavy-bottomed saucepan, stirring constantly; cook and stir at a boil until mixture is smooth, 3 to 5 minutes. Remove saucepan from heat; stir white chocolate chips and marshmallow creme into the sugar mixture until completely melted. Add vanilla extract; stir.
3. Gently fold 1/2 cup crumbled cookies into the white chocolate mixture until just incorporated; spread into the prepared pan. Sprinkle 1 cup crushed cookies evenly over the top. Press cookies lightly into the fudge. Cool at room temperature until set. Cut into small squares to serve.

SWEET CANDIED ORANGE AND LEMON PEEL
Servings: 12 | Prep: 10m | Cooks: 30m | Total: 4h40m

NUTRITION FACTS

Calories: 154 | Carbohydrates: 39.9g | Fat: 0g | Protein: 0.1g | Cholesterol: 0mg

INGREDIENTS

- 6 lemon peels, cut into 1/4 inch strips
- 1 cup water
- 4 orange peels, cut into 1/4 inch strips
- 1/3 cup white sugar for decoration
- 2 cups white sugar

DIRECTIONS

1. Place lemon and orange peel in large saucepan and cover with water. Bring to a boil over high heat. Boil for 20 minutes, drain and set aside.
2. In medium saucepan, combine 2 cups sugar and 1 cup water. Bring to a boil and cook until mixture reaches thread stage, 230 degrees F (108 degrees C) on candy thermometer, or small amount dropped in cold water forms a soft thread. Stir in peel, reduce heat and simmer 5 minutes, stirring frequently. Drain.
3. Roll peel pieces, a few at a time, in remaining sugar. Let dry on wire rack several hours. Store in airtight container.

EASY VEGAN PEANUT BUTTER FUDGE
Servings: 24 | Prep: 10m | Cooks: 5m | Total: 40m

NUTRITION FACTS

Calories: 188 | Carbohydrates: 21.2g | Fat: 11.1g | Protein: 2.8g | Cholesterol: 0mg

INGREDIENTS

- 3/4 cup vegan margarine
- 1 cup peanut butter
- 3 2/3 cups confectioners' sugar

DIRECTIONS

1. Lightly grease a 9x9 inch baking dish.
2. In a saucepan over low heat, melt margarine. Remove from heat and stir in peanut butter until smooth. Stir in confectioners' sugar, a little at a time, until well blended. Pat into prepared pan and chill until firm. Cut into squares.

HAROSET FOR PASSOVER
Servings: 6 | Prep: 20m | Cooks: 0m | Total: 20m

NUTRITION FACTS

Calories: 241 | Carbohydrates: 28.1g | Fat: 13.3g | Protein: 3.5g | Cholesterol: 0mg

INGREDIENTS

- 6 apples - peeled, cored and chopped
- 1 teaspoon white sugar
- 1 cup finely chopped walnuts
- 3 1/2 teaspoons honey
- 1/2 teaspoon ground cinnamon
- 1/3 cup sweet red wine

DIRECTIONS

1. Place the apples and walnuts into a large bowl. Mix together the cinnamon and sugar; sprinkle over the apples. Stir in the honey and sweet wine. Serve immediately, or refrigerate until serving.

GELATIN-FLAVORED POPCORN
Servings: 10 | Prep: 30m | Cooks: 15m | Total: 45m

NUTRITION FACTS

Calories: 323 | Carbohydrates: 29.2g | Fat: 23.2g | Protein: 1.7g | Cholesterol: 49mg

INGREDIENTS

- 10 cups popped popcorn
- 1 (3 ounce) package fruit flavored Jell-O mix
- 1 cup butter
- 1 tablespoon corn syrup
- 3/4 cup sugar
- 3 tablespoons water

DIRECTIONS

1. Preheat oven to 300 degrees F (150 degrees C). Grease a 1/4 sheet pan or two 8x12 inch baking dishes. Generously butter a heavy 2 quart saucepan.
2. Distribute popcorn evenly in prepared baking pans. Place in oven to keep warm.
3. In prepared saucepan over medium heat, combine butter, sugar, gelatin, corn syrup and water. Heat to 250 to 265 degrees F (121 to 129 degrees C), or until a small amount of syrup dropped into cold water forms a rigid ball.

4. Pour mixture evenly over popcorn and stir until coated. Return popcorn to oven and bake 5 minutes; stir, then bake 5 minutes more.
5. Turn popcorn out onto a large piece of foil. Let rest until cool enough to handle, then form into balls. Or let cool completely and break into clusters. Store in an airtight container, in a cool, dry place.

NEVER-NEVER EVER-EVER FAIL FUDGE
Servings: 64 | Prep: 15m | Cooks: 5m | Total: 1h

NUTRITION FACTS

Calories: 48 | Carbohydrates: 8.7g | Fat: 1.6g | Protein: 0.5g | Cholesterol: <1mg

INGREDIENTS

- 2/3 cup evaporated milk
- 1 cup semisweet chocolate chips
- 1 2/3 cups white sugar
- 1 teaspoon vanilla extract
- 1/2 teaspoon salt
- 1/2 cup chopped walnuts
- 16 large marshmallows

DIRECTIONS

1. In a medium saucepan over medium heat, combine evaporated milk, sugar and salt. Bring to a boil, then remove from heat and stir in marshmallows, chocolate chips, vanilla and nuts until marshmallows are melted. Pour into an 8x8 inch dish. Let cool completely before cutting into squares.

CANDIED LEMON PEEL
Servings: 15 | Prep: 10m | Cooks: 1h | Total: 1h40m

NUTRITION FACTS

Calories: 108 | Carbohydrates: 29g | Fat: 0.1g | Protein: 0.3g | Cholesterol: 0mg

INGREDIENTS

- 3 lemons
- 8 cups cold water, or as needed
- 2 cups white sugar, or as needed

DIRECTIONS

1. Cut lemons into slices about 1/4 inch thick and remove the fruit pulp. Cut the rings in half so the peels are in long strips.
2. Bring water and lemon peel to a boil in a small pan. Drain water, and repeat with fresh cold water. Repeat the boiling step three times (see Editor's Note). Drain and set peels aside.
3. Combine 2 cups fresh water with 2 cups sugar. Bring to a boil, stirring to dissolve the sugar. Reduce heat to low and stir in citrus peels; simmer until the white pith is translucent. Store peels in syrup, refrigerated, to keep them soft, or allow them to dry. Toss dry candied peels in additional sugar and store airtight at room temperature.

FAT PETE'S FUDGE
Servings: 72 | Prep: 10m | Cooks: 15m | Total: 1h25m

NUTRITION FACTS

Calories: 191 | Carbohydrates: 26.3g | Fat: 9.4g | Protein: 2.8g | Cholesterol: 8mg

INGREDIENTS

- 2/3 cup butter
- 16 ounces chocolate candy (such as Hershey's)
- 4 1/2 cups white sugar
- 2 1/2 cups milk chocolate chips
- 1 (12 fluid ounce) can evaporated milk
- 2 cups peanut butter (optional)
- 2 (7 ounce) jars marshmallow creme

DIRECTIONS

1. Grease a 9x13-inch baking pan. Set aside.
2. Bring butter, sugar, and evaporated milk to a boil in a saucepan over medium heat. Boil for 5 to 7 minutes, then remove from heat and quickly stir in the marshmallow cream, chocolate candy, and chocolate chips, until the chocolate has melted and is fully incorporated. Pour chocolate mixture into the prepared baking pan. Dot the top of the fudge with peanut butter. Swirl a knife through the fudge and peanut butter to create a marble effect. Cover and refrigerate until firm, about 1 hour. Cut into squares for serving.

CHOCOLATE ORANGE TRUFFLES
Servings: 12 | Prep: 40m | Cooks: 20m | Total: 5h30m

NUTRITION FACTS

Calories: 159 | Carbohydrates: 11.8g | Fat: 12.4g | Protein: 1.5g | Cholesterol: 15mg

INGREDIENTS

- 1/4 cup unsalted butter
- 1 teaspoon grated orange zest
- 3 tablespoons heavy cream
- 4 (1 ounce) squares semisweet chocolate, chopped
- 4 (1 ounce) squares semisweet chocolate, chopped
- 1 tablespoon vegetable oil
- 2 tablespoons orange liqueur

DIRECTIONS

1. In a medium saucepan over medium-high heat, combine butter and cream. Bring to a boil, and remove from heat. Stir in 4 ounces chopped chocolate, orange liqueur, and orange zest; continue stirring until smooth. Pour truffle mixture into a shallow bowl or a 9X5 in loaf pan. Chill until firm, about 2 hours.
2. Line a baking sheet with waxed paper. Shape chilled truffle mixture by rounded teaspoons into small balls (a melon baller also works well for this part). Place on prepared baking sheet. Chill until firm, about 30 minutes.
3. In the top of a double boiler over lightly simmering water, melt remaining 4 ounces chocolate with the oil, stirring until smooth. Cool to lukewarm.
4. Drop truffles, one at a time, into melted chocolate mixture. Using 2 forks, lift truffles out of the chocolate, allowing any excess chocolate to drip back into the pan before transferring back onto baking sheet. Chill until set.

CHOCOLATE SPIDERS

Servings: 20 | Prep: 5m | Cooks: 25m | Total: 30m

NUTRITION FACTS

Calories: 172 | Carbohydrates: 17.6g | Fat: 12.7g | Protein: 2.8g | Cholesterol: 0mg

INGREDIENTS

- 1 pound chocolate confectioners' coating
- 1 (8.5 ounce) package chow mein noodles

DIRECTIONS

1. Chop the chocolate confectioners' coating and place into a heatproof bowl over simmering water. Cook, stirring occasionally until melted and smooth. Remove from heat and stir in the chow mein noodles so they are evenly distributed. Spoon out to desired size onto waxed paper. Let cool completely before storing or serving.

CHOCOLATE-PEANUT BUTTER KETO CUPS

Servings: 12 | Prep: 15m | Cooks: 3m | Total: 1h18m

NUTRITION FACTS

Calories: 246 | Carbohydrates: 3.3g | Fat: 26g | Protein: 3.4g | Cholesterol: 3mg

INGREDIENTS

- 1 cup coconut oil
- 1 teaspoon liquid stevia
- 1/2 cup natural peanut butter
- 1/4 teaspoon vanilla extract
- 2 tablespoons heavy cream
- 1/4 teaspoon kosher salt
- 1 tablespoon cocoa powder
- 1 ounce chopped roasted salted peanuts

DIRECTIONS

1. Melt coconut oil in a saucepan over low heat, 3 to 5 minutes. Stir in peanut butter until smooth. Whisk in heavy cream, cocoa powder, liquid stevia, vanilla extract, and salt.
2. Pour chocolate-peanut butter mixture into 12 silicone muffin molds. Sprinkle peanuts evenly on top. Place molds on a baking sheet.
3. Freeze chocolate-peanut butter mixture until firm, at least 1 hour. Unmold chocolate-peanut cups and transfer to a resealable plastic bag or airtight container.

CHOCOLATE COVERED MARSHMALLOWS
Servings: 10 | Prep: 10m | Cooks: 5m | Total: 45m

NUTRITION FACTS

Calories: 184 | Carbohydrates: 27.1g | Fat: g | Protein: 1.5g | Cholesterol: 0mg

INGREDIENTS

- 2 cups semisweet chocolate chips
- 10 large marshmallows

DIRECTIONS

1. Melt the chocolate in a microwave-safe glass or ceramic bowl in 30-second intervals, stirring after each interval. Do not overheat or chocolate will scorch.
2. Dip the marshmallows in chocolate using a toothpick or fork to hold them. Place on waxed paper or aluminum foil, and freeze. Let marshmallows sit at room temperature for 5 minutes before serving.

PEPPERMINT MARSHMALLOWS
Servings: 40 | Prep: 25m | Cooks: 5m | Total: 4h30m

NUTRITION FACTS

Calories: 63 | Carbohydrates: 15.7g | Fat: 0g | Protein: 0.5g | Cholesterol: 0mg

INGREDIENTS

- 3/4 cup water, divided
- 2 teaspoons vanilla extract
- 3 (.25 ounce) packages unflavored gelatin
- 2 teaspoons peppermint extract
- 2/3 cup light corn syrup
- 1/4 cup cornstarch
- 2 cups white sugar
- 1/4 cup confectioners' sugar

DIRECTIONS

1. Line a 9x9 inch baking dish with lightly greased foil or plastic wrap. Grease another piece of foil or plastic wrap to cover the top, and set aside.
2. Place 1/2 cup of water in the bowl of an electric mixer, and sprinkle gelatin on top of water to soak.
3. While gelatin is soaking, combine 1/4 cup of water, corn syrup, and sugar in a saucepan, and bring to a boil over medium heat. Boil the mixture hard for 1 minute.
4. Pour the hot sugar mixture into the gelatin mixture and beat on high for 12 minutes with electric mixer, until the mixture is fluffy and forms stiff peaks. Add vanilla and peppermint extracts, and beat just until blended.
5. Pour the marshmallow mixture into the prepared baking dish, using a greased spatula to smooth the top of the candy. Cover the candy with the reserved greased foil or wrap, and press down lightly to seal the covering to the top of the candy.
6. Allow the marshmallow candy to rest for 4 hours or overnight. Mix together cornstarch and confectioner's sugar in a shallow dish. Using oiled scissors or an oiled kitchen knife, cut the marshmallow candy into strips, then into 1 inch squares. Dredge the marshmallows lightly in the cornstarch mixture and store in an airtight container.

CATHY'S PEANUT BUTTER FUDGE
Servings: 12 | Prep: 25m | Cooks: 0m | Total: 25m

NUTRITION FACTS

Calories: 281 | Carbohydrates: 40.9g | Fat: 12g | Protein: 5.8g | Cholesterol: 3mg

INGREDIENTS

- 2 cups packed brown sugar
- 1 tablespoon water
- 1 tablespoon butter
- 1 teaspoon vanilla extract

- 1/2 cup milk
- 1 cup creamy peanut butter
- 1 teaspoon cornstarch

DIRECTIONS

1. Grease an 8x8 inch square pan.
2. In a saucepan over medium heat, combine the brown sugar , butter and milk. cook until the mixture reaches the soft ball stage (234-240 degrees F, 112-115 degrees C).
3. Combine the cornstarch and water, add to the saucepan and mix well. Remove from heat and beat for 2 minutes. Stir in the vanilla and peanut butter until thoroughly blended. Spread batter evenly into the prepared pan. let cool, then cut into squares and enjoy.

AMAZING HEALTHY DARK CHOCOLATE
Servings: 24 | Prep: 5m | Cooks: 0m | Total: 5m

NUTRITION FACTS

Calories: 121 | Carbohydrates: 10.8g | Fat: 9.6g | Protein: 0.7g | Cholesterol: 0mg

INGREDIENTS

- 1 cup coconut oil, melted
- 1 cup unsweetened cocoa powder
- 1 cup maple syrup

DIRECTIONS

1. Mix coconut oil, cocoa powder, and maple syrup together in a bowl until evenly combined.

SOFT CARAMEL CORN
Servings: 40 | Prep: 5m | Cooks: 15m | Total: 30m

NUTRITION FACTS

Calories: 159 | Carbohydrates: 24.6g | Fat: 7g | Protein: 1g | Cholesterol: 13mg

INGREDIENTS

- 3 (3.5 ounce) packages microwave popcorn, popped
- 1 cup butter
- 2 1/4 cups packed brown sugar
- 1 (5 ounce) can sweetened condensed milk
- 1 cup corn syrup

DIRECTIONS

1. Place the popcorn in a large bowl. Shake and toss the bowl to make the unpopped kernels go to the bottom; discard.
2. In a sauce pan over medium-high heat, cook the brown sugar, corn syrup, and butter, stirring constantly. Heat to 270 to 290 degrees F (132 to 143 degrees C), or until a small amount of syrup dropped into cold water forms hard but pliable threads. Remove from the heat, and carefully pour in the can of condensed milk; stir until smooth.
3. Pour 1/4 of the caramel at a time over the popcorn, stirring until all of the popcorn is covered. Cool at least 10 minutes before serving.

MINT CHOCOLATE FUDGE

Servings: 28 | Prep: 10m | Cooks: 15m | Total: 45m

NUTRITION FACTS

Calories: 137 | Carbohydrates: 18.8g | Fat: 6.8g | Protein: 2g | Cholesterol: 6mg

INGREDIENTS

- 2 cups semisweet chocolate chips
- 1 cup white confectioners' coating
- 1 (14 ounce) can sweetened condensed milk, divided
- 1 tablespoon peppermint extract
- 2 teaspoons vanilla extract
- 1 drop green food coloring (optional)

DIRECTIONS

1. Line an 8 or 9 inch square pan with waxed paper.
2. In heavy saucepan over low heat, melt chocolate chips with 1 cup sweetened condensed milk and vanilla. Spread half of the mixture into prepared pan; chill 10 minutes, or until firm. Reserve remaining chocolate mixture at room temperature.
3. In another heavy saucepan over low heat, melt white confectioners' coating with remaining sweetened condensed milk (mixture will be thick.) Stir in peppermint extract and food coloring. Spread this mixture on chilled chocolate layer; chill 10 minutes, or until firm.
4. Spread reserved chocolate mixture over the mint layer; chill 2 hours, or until firm.

CANDY BAR FUDGE

Servings: 32 | Prep: 20m | Cooks: 10m | Total: 2h30m

NUTRITION FACTS

Calories: 205 | Carbohydrates: 28.4g | Fat: 10g | Protein: 3.2g | Cholesterol: 9mg

INGREDIENTS

- 1/2 cup butter
- 30 individually wrapped caramels, unwrapped
- 1/3 cup unsweetened cocoa powder
- 1 tablespoon water
- 1/4 cup packed brown sugar
- 2 cups salted peanuts
- 1/4 cup milk
- 1/2 cup semisweet chocolate chips
- 3 1/2 cups confectioners' sugar
- 1/2 cup milk chocolate chips
- 1 teaspoon vanilla extract

DIRECTIONS

1. Grease an 8x8 inch square baking pan.
2. In a microwave-safe bowl, combine butter, cocoa powder, brown sugar and milk. Microwave until mixture boils. Stir in confectioners' sugar and vanilla extract. Pour into prepared pan.
3. In a microwave-safe bowl, microwave caramels and water until caramels melt. Stir in peanuts. Spread mixture over chocolate layer.
4. In a small microwave-safe bowl, combine semisweet and milk chocolate chips; microwave until melted. Spread over caramel layer. Chill for 2 hours, or until firm.

ESPRESSO BARK

Servings: 12 | Prep: 10m | Cooks: 15m | Total: 25m

NUTRITION FACTS

Calories: 160 | Carbohydrates: 20.4g | Fat: 9.9g | Protein: 1.5g | Cholesterol: <1mg

INGREDIENTS

- 2 cups semisweet chocolate chips
- 3/4 cup whole coffee beans
- 1 teaspoon margarine
- 1/4 cup chopped white chocolate

DIRECTIONS

1. Cover a cookie sheet with waxed paper.
2. Combine the chocolate chips and margarine in a microwave-safe bowl. Heat in the microwave at 30 second intervals, stirring between each, until melted and smooth. Mix in the coffee beans until evenly distributed.

3. Pour the chocolate out onto the waxed paper and spread into an even layer. Sprinkle the pieces of white chocolate evenly over the top and press in lightly to make sure they stick. Place in the freezer until set, about 5 minutes. Break into pieces and store in an airtight container.

CREAM CHEESE CANDIES
Servings: 72 | Prep: 20m | Cooks: 1h | Total: 1h20m | Additional: 1h

NUTRITION FACTS

Calories: 24 | Carbohydrates: 5g | Fat: 0.4g | Protein: 0.1g | Cholesterol: 1mg

INGREDIENTS

- 1 (3 ounce) package cream cheese, softened
- 1/4 teaspoon peppermint extract
- 3 cups confectioners' sugar

DIRECTIONS

1. In a small mixing bowl, beat cream cheese with peppermint extract. Beat in half the confectioners' sugar until smooth. Knead in remaining confectioners' sugar until fully incorporated. Shape dough into 1/2 inch balls, place on baking sheets, flatten with a fork, and allow to stand 1 hour to harden. Store in airtight containers in refrigerator.

SWEETENED POPCORN
Servings: 12 | Prep: 15m | Cooks: 10m | Total: 25m

NUTRITION FACTS

Calories: 101 | Carbohydrates: 18.9g | Fat: 3.1g | Protein: 0.3g | Cholesterol: 5mg

INGREDIENTS

- 2 tablespoons butter
- 1 cup white sugar
- 1/4 cup water
- 6 cups popped butter flavor popcorn

DIRECTIONS

1. Line two baking sheets with waxed paper.
2. In a large pot or Dutch oven, combine butter, water and sugar. Bring to a boil. Boil 4 minutes; remove from heat. Introduce popcorn and stir to coat evenly. Pour onto prepared baking sheets and let cool before serving.

LIP-SMACKING POPCORN CONCOCTION
Servings: 20 | Prep: 20m | Cooks: 3m | Total: 23m

NUTRITION FACTS

Calories: 317 | Carbohydrates: 36.5g | Fat: 16.8g | Protein: 5.6g | Cholesterol: 5mg

INGREDIENTS

- 2 envelopes microwave popcorn without butter, popped
- 2 (2.25 ounce) packages blanched slivered almonds
- 4 cups corn cereal puffs (e.g. Kix™)
- 2 cups thin pretzel sticks
- 1 (10.5 ounce) bag extruded corn chips (e.g. Fritos™)
- 1 pound vanilla flavored confectioners' coating

DIRECTIONS

1. Cover a large flat surface with waxed paper. In a large bowl, stir together the popcorn, cereal, corn chips, almonds, and pretzels.
2. Melt the confectioners' coating in a glass bowl in the microwave for 1 minute. Continue to cook at 30 second intervals, stirring between each one, until the coating is smooth.
3. Pour melted coating over the cereal mixture. It's best to use a large metal spoon, and pour 1 or 2 spoonfuls at a time then mix to ensure even distribution. (A second person can be useful here - one to pour, one to mix.) Once everything is coated, spread the mixture out onto waxed paper in a thin layer. Let stand for about 1/2 hour, or until coating is dry. Transfer to a bowl to serve, or store in an airtight container.

PEPPERMINT BARK
Servings: 24 | Prep: 20m | Cooks: 20m | Total: 1h40m

NUTRITION FACTS

Calories: 330 | Carbohydrates: 40.9g | Fat: 18.1g | Protein: 3g | Cholesterol: 13mg

INGREDIENTS

- 30 crushed peppermint hard candies, divided
- 1 1/2 pounds white chocolate, chopped
- 1 1/2 pounds milk chocolate candy, coarsely chopped
- 1 teaspoon oil-based peppermint flavoring, or to taste

DIRECTIONS

1. Spread 1/3 of the peppermint candy over a 9x13-inch baking pan lined with wax paper.

2. Melt the milk chocolate in the top of a double boiler over just-barely simmering water, stirring frequently and scraping down the sides with a rubber spatula to avoid scorching, just until melted. Pour the melted chocolate over peppermint candy in the prepared pan. Sprinkle another 1/3 of the candy on top of the milk chocolate. Refrigerate until the chocolate hardens, about 30 minutes.
3. Melt the white chocolate in the top of a double boiler over just-barely simmering water, stirring frequently and scraping down the sides with a rubber spatula to avoid scorching. Stir in the oil-based peppermint flavoring. Pour the white chocolate over the milk chocolate, then spread the remaining 1/3 peppermint candy on top.
4. Refrigerate until the white chocolate hardens, about 30 minutes. Cut or break into pieces to serve.

JELLYBEAN BARK
Servings: 16 | Prep: 10m | Cooks: 5m | Total: 1h15m

NUTRITION FACTS

Calories: 259 | Carbohydrates: 43.4g | Fat: 9.1g | Protein: 1.7g | Cholesterol: 6mg

INGREDIENTS

- 1 pound white confectioners' coating
- 1 pound jellybeans

DIRECTIONS

1. Line a jelly roll pan with waxed paper and set aside.
2. Melt the white confectioners' coating in the top of a double boiler over just-barely simmering water, stirring frequently and scraping down the sides with a rubber spatula to avoid scorching. Spread the melted white confectioners' coating onto the prepared pan. Sprinkle the jellybeans over the top.
3. Refrigerate at least 1 hour or until firm. Break into pieces to serve.

CHOCOLATE PRETZEL TREATS
Servings: 40 | Prep: 10m | Cooks: 2m | Total: 22m

NUTRITION FACTS

Calories: 36 | Carbohydrates: 4.5g | Fat: 2g | Protein: 0.5g | Cholesterol: 1mg

INGREDIENTS

- 1 (15 ounce) package small pretzel twists
- 1 (8 ounce) package milk chocolate candy kisses (such as Hershey's Kisses), unwrapped
- 1 (1.69 ounce) package candy-coated milk chocolate pieces (such as M&M's)

DIRECTIONS

1. Preheat oven to 175 degrees F (80 degrees C).

2. Arrange pretzels on a baking sheet. Place a candy kiss on the center of each pretzel.
3. Warm pretzels in the preheated oven until candy kiss is shiny and slightly softened, 2 minutes.
4. Place a candy-coated chocolate piece atop the candy kiss on each pretzel; press down. Chill in the refrigerator for 10 minutes.

PEANUT BUTTER FUDGE WITH MARSHMALLOW CREME

Servings: 24 | Prep: 5m | Cooks: 10m | Total: 50m

NUTRITION FACTS

Calories: 254 | Carbohydrates: 39.9g | Fat: 10g | Protein: 3.5g | Cholesterol: 3mg

INGREDIENTS

- 4 cups white sugar
- 1 cup peanut butter
- 1 cup evaporated milk
- 1 cup marshmallow creme
- 1/2 cup margarine

DIRECTIONS

1. Line a 9x13 inch pan with foil or parchment paper.
2. In a medium saucepan, combine the sugar, evaporated milk and butter. Cook over medium heat stirring frequently until it comes to a boil. Boil for 10 minutes, remove from heat and stir in peanut butter and marshmallow creme. Pour into the prepared pan and chill until set. Cut into squares and serve.

PEANUT BUTTER CUPS

Servings: 12 | Prep: 10m | Cooks: 5m | Total: 45m

NUTRITION FACTS

Calories: 143 | Carbohydrates: 9.9g | Fat: 11.9g | Protein: 2g | Cholesterol: 10mg

INGREDIENTS

- 1 cup semisweet chocolate chips
- 1 tablespoon vegetable oil
- 1/4 cup butter
- 1/4 cup peanut butter

DIRECTIONS

1. Coat a small cup muffin tin with cooking spray. In a microwave-safe bowl, microwave chocolate with butter and oil, stirring often, until melted, 1 to 2 minutes. Pour about a tablespoon of the chocolate mixture into each muffin cup.
2. Melt peanut butter in microwave, 30 to 40 seconds. Spoon about 1 teaspoon of melted peanut butter over chocolate in each muffin cup. Top with another tablespoon of chocolate.
3. Chill in refrigerator 30 minutes, until set.

FAMOUS COCONUT-ALMOND BALLS
Servings: 13 | Prep: 15m | Cooks: 15m | Total: 30m

NUTRITION FACTS

Calories: 379 | Carbohydrates: 28.4g | Fat: 31.4g | Protein: 3.6g | Cholesterol: 0mg

INGREDIENTS

- 4 cups flaked coconut
- 1/4 cup shortening
- 1/4 cup light corn syrup
- 26 whole almonds
- 1 (12 ounce) package semisweet chocolate chips

DIRECTIONS

1. Line two cookie sheets or large flat surface with waxed paper and place large cooling rack on top. Place coconut in large bowl. Heat corn syrup, one minute in microwave, until syrup boils. Pour immediately over coconut and stir until well mixed.
2. Using a tablespoon measure, shape coconut into 26 balls with hands and place on wire racks. Let rest 10 minutes, then re-roll each ball to keep loose ends from sticking out.
3. Melt shortening and chocolate together in large glass bowl in microwave, or in saucepan on stovetop, stirring once or twice. Working quickly, spoon 1 tablespoon of chocolate over each ball. Lightly press an almond on top of each ball. Let balls stand until set.

GA GA CLUSTERS
Servings: 12 | Prep: 5m | Cooks: 5m | Total: 2h10m

NUTRITION FACTS

Calories: 500 | Carbohydrates: 71g | Fat: 23.4g | Protein: 10.2g | Cholesterol: 11mg

INGREDIENTS

- 1 (12 ounce) package semisweet chocolate chips
- 1 (16 ounce) package miniature marshmallows
- 1 (14 ounce) can sweetened condensed milk

- 2 cups dry roasted peanuts

DIRECTIONS

1. Lightly grease a 9x13 inch baking dish. In a medium saucepan over low heat combine chocolate chips and milk and stir until chips are melted and mixture is smooth. Meanwhile, combine the marshmallows and peanuts in a large bowl.
2. When chocolate mixture is heated, pour melted mixture over marshmallows and nuts and mix all together. Pour mixture into the baking dish, cover and refrigerate to chill for 2 hours.

EASY MICROWAVE PRALINES
Servings: 18 | Prep: 20m | Cooks: 13m | Total: 35m

NUTRITION FACTS

Calories: 239 | Carbohydrates: 28.5g | Fat: 14.4g | Protein: 1.4g | Cholesterol: 20mg

INGREDIENTS

- 1 pound light brown sugar
- 1 tablespoon butter
- 1 cup heavy whipping cream
- 2 cups chopped toasted pecans
- 2 tablespoons light corn syrup

DIRECTIONS

1. In a deep, microwave-safe bowl, mix together brown sugar, whipping cream, and corn syrup. Microwave on High for 13 minutes.
2. Mix in butter until well blended. Then stir, stir, and stir until mixture begins to cool and get creamy. Stir in chopped nuts. Drop by tablespoonfuls onto waxed paper to cool.

CARAMEL CANDIES
Servings: 12 | Prep: 25m | Cooks: 20m | Total: 45m

NUTRITION FACTS

Calories: 504 | Carbohydrates: 72.7g | Fat: 25g | Protein: 1.2g | Cholesterol: 76mg

INGREDIENTS

- 1 1/4 cups brown sugar
- 1 1/4 cups heavy cream
- 1 2/3 cups white sugar
- 3/4 cup whole milk

- 1 cup butter
- 2 teaspoons vanilla extract
- 1 cup corn syrup

DIRECTIONS

1. Combine brown sugar, white sugar, butter, corn syrup, cream, milk and vanilla in a medium saucepan over medium heat. Heat, stirring occasionally, to 250 to 265 degrees F (121 to 129 degrees C), or until a small amount of syrup dropped into cold water forms a rigid ball. Pour into an 8x8 inch pan. Let cool before cutting.

CREAMY EGGNOG FUDGE
Servings: 64 | Prep: 5m | Cooks: 15m | Total: 20m

NUTRITION FACTS

Calories: 89 | Carbohydrates: 12.3g | Fat: 4.4g | Protein: 0.5g | Cholesterol: 8mg

INGREDIENTS

- 2 cups white sugar
- 12 ounces white chocolate, chopped
- 3/4 cup butter
- 1 (7 ounce) jar marshmallow cream
- 2/3 cup eggnog
- 1 teaspoon vanilla extract
- 2 teaspoons ground nutmeg
- 1/4 cup chopped walnuts
- 1 teaspoon ground cinnamon

DIRECTIONS

1. Grease a 9 inch square pan and set aside.
2. Combine the sugar, butter, eggnog, nutmeg, and cinnamon in a large saucepan. Bring to a boil, stirring occasionally to melt the butter. Once the mixture reaches a rolling boil, stop stirring, and clip a candy thermometer onto the pan.
3. Heat mixture to 235 degrees F (113 degrees C), or until a small amount of syrup dropped into cold water forms a soft ball that flattens when removed from the water and placed on a flat surface.
4. Remove the pan from the heat and stir in the white chocolate pieces, marshmallow cream, vanilla, and walnuts. Beat the mixture with a wooden spoon until fluffy and it starts to lose its gloss. Spoon into the prepared pan, spreading evenly. Cool completely, then cut into small squares for serving.

BROWN SUGAR FUDGE
Servings: 64 | Prep: 15m | Cooks: 10m | Total: 55m

NUTRITION FACTS

Calories: 82 | Carbohydrates: 11.1g | Fat: 4.3g | Protein: 0.5g | Cholesterol: 8mg

INGREDIENTS

- 3 cups brown sugar
- 2 cups confectioners' sugar
- 3/4 cup evaporated milk
- 1 cup chopped walnuts (optional)
- 1 cup butter

DIRECTIONS

1. Grease an 8x8-inch pan.
2. Bring brown sugar, evaporated milk, and butter to a boil in a large saucepan; boil mixture for exactly 10 minutes. Remove from heat and add confectioners' sugar. Beat fudge with an electric mixer on medium speed for exactly 5 minutes. Stir in walnuts. Spread fudge into the prepared pan and let cool before cutting into squares.

TIGER BUTTER

Servings: 12 | Prep: 1 | Cooks: 3m | Total: 30m

NUTRITION FACTS

Calories: 267 | Carbohydrates: 27.2g | Fat: 16.8g | Protein: 4.2g | Cholesterol: 8mg

INGREDIENTS

- 1 pound white chocolate, chopped
- 1/3 cup crunchy peanut butter
- 1/4 cup semisweet chocolate chips
- 1/2 cup crispy rice cereal

DIRECTIONS

1. Line a 9x9 inch dish with waxed paper.
2. Combine white chocolate, chocolate chips and peanut butter in a 2 quart microwave safe dish and microwave on low one minute. Stir until smooth. Stir in the rice cereal and spread into prepared pan. Let cool completely before cutting into squares.

EASY CINNAMON FUDGE

Servings: 32 | Prep: 10m | Cooks: 10m | Total: 1h20m

NUTRITION FACTS

Calories: 100 | Carbohydrates: 13.1g | Fat: 5.5g | Protein: 0.9g | Cholesterol: 8mg

INGREDIENTS

- 3 cups confectioners' sugar
- 1/4 cup milk
- 1/2 cup unsweetened cocoa powder
- 1 1/2 teaspoons vanilla extract
- 1/2 teaspoon ground cinnamon
- 1 cup chopped walnuts (optional)
- 1/2 cup butter

DIRECTIONS

1. Line an 8x8 inch baking pan with aluminum foil, allowing foil to hang over the edges. Grease the foil.
2. In a medium bowl combine confectioners' sugar, cocoa and cinnamon.
3. Heat butter and milk in a medium saucepan over medium heat. When butter is melted stir in vanilla. Remove from heat and stir in sugar mixture and walnuts.
4. Pour into prepared pan. Refrigerate for 1 hour, or until firm.
5. Lift foil out of pan. Cut fudge into 2 inch squares, and then cut in half diagonally to make triangles.

CHOCOLATE COVERED CHERRIES
Servings: 16 | Prep: 45m | Cooks: 4h | Total: 4h45m

NUTRITION FACTS

Calories: 249 | Carbohydrates: 41.1g | Fat: 10.8g | Protein: 1g | Cholesterol: <1mg

INGREDIENTS

- 2 1/2 cups confectioners' sugar
- 4 (4 ounce) jars maraschino cherries, drained
- 1/4 cup margarine
- 2 cups semisweet chocolate chips
- 1 tablespoon milk
- 2 tablespoons shortening
- 1/2 teaspoon almond extract

DIRECTIONS

1. In a medium bowl, mix together confectioner's sugar, margarine, milk and almond extract.
2. On a lightly floured surface, knead the mixture into a large ball. Roll into 1 inch balls. Flatten the balls into 2 inch circles. Leaving the stems sticking out, wrap the cherries in the circles by lightly

rolling in hands. Place the wrapped cherries on wax paper and chill in the refrigerator at least 4 hours.

3. In a medium saucepan over medium heat, melt chocolate chips and shortening. Holding by the stem, dip the chilled cherries into the chocolate chip mixture. Chill until serving.

HOMEMADE MARSHMALLOWS
Servings: 24 | Prep: 30m | Cooks: 12m | Total: 8h

NUTRITION FACTS

Calories: 128 | Carbohydrates: 32.9g | Fat: 0g | Protein: 0g | Cholesterol: 0mg

INGREDIENTS

- 3 cups white sugar
- 3/4 cup water
- 1/4 cup corn syrup
- 2 teaspoons vanilla extract
- 1/4 teaspoon salt
- 1 cup confectioners' sugar for dusting

DIRECTIONS

1. Generously coat a 9x13 dish with cooking spray.
2. In a large saucepan, combine sugar, corn syrup, salt and water. Heat to between 234 and 240 degrees F (112 to 116 degrees C), or until a small amount of syrup dropped into cold water forms a soft ball that flattens when removed from the water and placed on a flat surface. Remove from heat and beat with an electric mixer until stiff peaks form, 10 to 12 minutes. Stir in vanilla. Pour into prepared pan.
3. Chill in refrigerator 8 hours or overnight. To cut, loosen edges with a knife. Dust surface with confectioners' sugar, and turn out onto a waxed paper lined surface. Dust with confectioners' sugar again and cut with a knife.

SWEDISH CHOCOLATE BALLS (OR COCONUT BALLS)
Servings: 48 | Prep: 20m | Cooks: 2h | Total: 2h20m

NUTRITION FACTS

Calories: 90 | Carbohydrates: 10.9g | Fat: 5.2g | Protein: 1.3g | Cholesterol: 10mg

INGREDIENTS

- 4 cups regular rolled oats
- 2 tablespoons strong coffee
- 1 1/4 cups white sugar
- 1 teaspoon vanilla extract

- 1/2 cup unsweetened cocoa powder
- 2 (1 ounce) squares unsweetened baking chocolate, melted
- 1 cup butter or margarine, softened
- 1/3 cup coconut flakes

DIRECTIONS

1. Mix the oats, sugar, and cocoa together in a bowl. Add the butter, and use your hands to mix the ingredients together to make a thick dough. Mix in the coffee, vanilla, and chocolate until thoroughly blended.
2. Place the coconut flakes in a small bowl. Pinch off small amounts of dough and roll between your hands to make small balls, about 1-1/2 inches in diameter. Roll the balls in the coconut flakes. Balls are ready to eat, or may be refrigerated 2 hours to become firmer.

GOURMET PRETZEL RODS
Servings: 15 | Prep: 5m | Cooks: 10m | Total: 15m

NUTRITION FACTS

Calories: 287 | Carbohydrates: 40g | Fat: 12.5g | Protein: 6.2g | Cholesterol: 4mg

INGREDIENTS

- 1 (14 ounce) package individually wrapped caramels, unwrapped
- 1/2 (14 ounce) package candy-coated chocolate pieces
- 1 tablespoon water
- 1 1/2 cups chopped peanuts
- 15 pretzel rods

DIRECTIONS

1. In a microwave safe dish, combine caramels and water. Microwave for 2 to 2 1/2 minutes or until smooth, stirring after each minute.
2. Dip a pretzel rod into melted caramel. Reserve about an inch at the end to use as a handle, and spread smooth with a spatula or the back of a spoon. Attach 12 chocolate pieces, then roll in chopped peanuts. Place on wax paper until set.

PEANUT BUTTER POTATO CANDY
Servings: 20 | Prep: 20m | Cooks: 2h | Total: 2h20m

NUTRITION FACTS

Calories: 117 | Carbohydrates: 24g | Fat: 2.2g | Protein: 1.2g | Cholesterol: <1mg

INGREDIENTS

- 1/4 cup mashed potatoes
- 1 (16 ounce) package confectioners' sugar
- 2 tablespoons milk
- 1 tablespoon confectioners' sugar for dusting, or as needed
- 1 teaspoon vanilla extract
- 1/3 cup peanut butter, or as needed
- 1 pinch salt

DIRECTIONS

1. Combine mashed potatoes, milk, vanilla extract, and salt in a bowl.
2. Stir confectioners' sugar into potato mixture until a dough consistency is reached. Refrigerate dough until chilled, about 1 hour.
3. Sprinkle confectioners' sugar on a cutting board or waxed paper.
4. Roll dough into a large rectangular shape on prepared surface.
5. Spread enough peanut butter on top layer of dough to cover.
6. Roll dough into a jelly roll shape; refrigerate roll for 1 hour. Slice dough into pinwheels to serve.

S'MORES

Servings: 1 | Prep: 1m | Cooks: 2m | Total: 3m

NUTRITION FACTS

Calories: 277 | Carbohydrates: 37.8g | Fat: 14g | Protein: 2.7g | Cholesterol: 10mg

INGREDIENTS

- 1 large marshmallow
- 1 graham cracker
- 1 (1.5 ounce) bar chocolate candy bar

DIRECTIONS

1. Heat the marshmallow over an open flame until it begins to brown and melt.
2. Break the graham cracker in half. Sandwich the chocolate between the cracker and the hot marshmallow. Allow the marshmallow to cool a moment before eating.

CRISPY MARSHMALLOW BALLS

Servings: 48 | Prep: 20m | Cooks: 10m | Total: 45m

NUTRITION FACTS

Calories: 122 | Carbohydrates: 18.9g | Fat: 5g | Protein: 1.3g | Cholesterol: 3mg

INGREDIENTS

- 4 cups crispy rice cereal
- 30 individually wrapped caramels, unwrapped
- 1 (14 ounce) can sweetened condensed milk
- 1 (16 ounce) package large marshmallows
- 1 cup margarine

DIRECTIONS

1. Line trays with waxed paper. Pour rice cereal into a shallow dish or bowl.
2. In a double boiler, combine condensed milk, margarine and caramels. Cook, stirring, over simmering water, until melted and smooth.
3. Using tongs or two forks, dip marshmallows one at a time into caramel mixture, then roll in rice cereal. Place on waxed paper until set.

CARAMEL CHOCOLATE CORN
Servings: 32 | Prep: 7m | Cooks: 8m | Total: 30m

NUTRITION FACTS

Calories: 147 | Carbohydrates: 15.3g | Fat: 9.4g | Protein: 1.9g | Cholesterol: 9mg

INGREDIENTS

- 16 cups popped popcorn
- 1 teaspoon vanilla extract
- 1 cup roasted peanuts
- 1 teaspoon salt
- 1 cup brown sugar
- 1/2 teaspoon baking soda
- 1/2 cup butter
- 1 cup milk chocolate chips
- 1/4 cup light corn syrup
- 1 teaspoon shortening

DIRECTIONS

1. Grease cookie sheets.
2. Place popcorn and peanuts in a paper bag. Set aside.
3. In a microwave safe bowl, combine sugar, butter, corn syrup, vanilla and salt. Microwave 4 minutes, until bubbly. Stir in baking soda. Pour over popcorn mixture and shake bag to coat.
4. Roll down edges of bag and place bag in microwave. Heat for 2 minutes, shaking three times to mix. Spread mixture onto prepared sheets to cool.
5. In a microwave safe bowl, combine chocolate and shortening. Microwave 90 seconds, stirring once, until melted. Drizzle over popcorn mixture. Let cool before serving.

EGGNOG FUDGE

Servings: 24 | Prep: 15m | Cooks: 10m | Total: 2h25m

NUTRITION FACTS

Calories: 190 | Carbohydrates: 33.5g | Fat: 6g | Protein: 1.7g | Cholesterol: 10mg

INGREDIENTS

- 1 cooking spray
- 1/2 teaspoon ground nutmeg
- 1 cup eggnog
- 1/8 cup butter, chilled
- 3 cups white sugar
- 1/2 (11 ounce) package white chocolate chips
- 1 1/2 cups miniature marshmallows
- 1 cup chopped almonds
- 1/2 teaspoon ground cinnamon

DIRECTIONS

1. Line a 9 x 13 inch baking pan with aluminum foil and set aside.
2. Spray the bottom and sides of a large saucepan with cooking spray. Heat eggnog and sugar over medium heat. Bring to rolling boil, stirring constantly with a wooden spoon. Boil for 2 minutes.
3. Fold in marshmallows, cinnamon and nutmeg. Return to a boil for 6 minutes, stirring constantly. As the mixture boils it will become brown. Remove from heat and quickly stir in butter, white chocolate chips and almonds. Stir until well mixed and glossy.
4. Quickly pour into prepared pan.
5. Cool at room temperature. Remove from pan, remove foil and cut into squares.

NAT'S BUTTERY CASHEW CRUNCH

Servings: 24 | Prep: 5m | Cooks: 15m | Total: 19m

NUTRITION FACTS

Calories: 178 | Carbohydrates: 14.9g | Fat: 13.1g | Protein: 1.9g | Cholesterol: 20mg

INGREDIENTS

- 1 cup unsalted butter
- 1 tablespoon light corn syrup
- 1 1/4 cups white sugar
- 10 ounces cashews
- 1/4 teaspoon salt

DIRECTIONS

1. Generously butter or grease a large baking sheet, and set aside.
2. In a saucepan over medium heat, combine the butter, sugar, salt and corn syrup. Cook, stirring until butter is melted. Stir in the cashews, and increase the heat to high. Heat to 300 to 310 degrees F (149 to 154 degrees C), or until a small amount of syrup dropped into cold water forms hard, brittle threads. Stir occasionally with a long handled wooden spoon so the cashews do not burn.
3. Pour onto a greased baking sheet, and allow to cool for about 10 minutes. Break into pieces, and store in an airtight container lined with waxed paper.

BAVARIAN MINTS
Servings: 25 | Prep: 15m | Cooks: 25m | Total: 40m

NUTRITION FACTS

Calories: 168 | Carbohydrates: 21g | Fat: 9.1g | Protein: 2.7g | Cholesterol: 13mg

INGREDIENTS

- 3 cups milk chocolate chips
- 1 (14 ounce) can sweetened condensed milk
- 1 (1 ounce) square unsweetened chocolate, chopped
- 1 teaspoon peppermint extract
- 1 tablespoon butter
- 1 teaspoon vanilla extract

DIRECTIONS

1. Butter an 8x8 inch dish.
2. In a medium saucepan over low heat, combine milk chocolate chips, unsweetened chocolate and butter. Heat until melted and smooth, stirring occasionally. Remove from heat and stir in condensed milk, peppermint extract and vanilla extract.
3. Beat with an electric mixer at a low speed for 1 minute, then at a high speed for 1 minute. Chill mixture for 15 minutes, beating by hand every 5 minutes. Beat again with electric mixer two minutes more. Pour into prepared pan and chill until firm. Cut into 1/2 inch squares.

LICORICE CARAMELS
Servings: 64 | Prep: 10m | Cooks: 30m | Total: 3h

NUTRITION FACTS

Calories: 84 | Carbohydrates: 13.5g | Fat: 3.4g | Protein: 0.5g | Cholesterol: 10mg

INGREDIENTS

- 1 cup butter
- 1/8 teaspoon salt
- 2 cups white sugar
- 1 teaspoon anise extract
- 1 (14 ounce) can sweetened condensed milk
- black paste food coloring
- 1 cup corn syrup

DIRECTIONS

1. Line a 9x9 inch dish with buttered foil.
2. In a large saucepan over medium heat, melt butter. Stir in sugar, milk, corn syrup and salt. Bring to a boil, stirring frequently. Continue to heat, without stirring, to 242 to 248 degrees F (116 to 120 degrees C), or until a small amount of syrup dropped into cold water forms a firm but pliable ball. Remove from heat and stir in anise and food coloring. Pour into prepared pan. Let cool completely, several hours.
3. To cut, turn out of pan and peel away foil. Cut with a buttered knife. Wrap pieces in waxed paper or candy wrappers.

CHOCOLATE ORANGE FUDGE
Servings: 20 | Prep: 5m | Cooks: 5m | Total: 2h10m

NUTRITION FACTS

Calories: 183 | Carbohydrates: 24.3g | Fat: 10g | Protein: 2.7g | Cholesterol: 7mg

INGREDIENTS

- 2 1/2 cups semisweet chocolate chips
- 1/2 cup chopped pecans
- 1 (14 ounce) can sweetened condensed milk
- 2 teaspoons grated orange peel

DIRECTIONS

1. Line an 8 x 8 inch square pan with parchment paper.
2. Melt chocolate chips with condensed milk in the top of a double boiler or in a bowl in the microwave. Stir until smooth. Remove from heat and stir in pecans and grated orange peel.
3. Pour chocolate mixture into prepared pan. Chill 2 hours, or until firm, and cut into squares. Store, covered, in the refrigerator.

EASTER EGG NESTS
Servings: 12 | Prep: 30m | Cooks: 5m | Total: 35m

NUTRITION FACTS

Calories: 113 | Carbohydrates: 12.6g | Fat: 6.8g | Protein: 1.1g | Cholesterol: 3mg

INGREDIENTS

- 3 drops green food coloring
- 1 1/3 cups flaked coconut
- 1/2 teaspoon milk
- 6 ounces white confectioners' coating

DIRECTIONS

1. In a small bowl, mix food coloring with milk; add coconut and mix until evenly tinted; set aside.
2. Melt confectioners' coating over a double boiler or in the microwave, stirring every 15 to 30 seconds until smooth. Mix with coconut mixture and place by spoonfuls on waxed paper. Shape mixture like a bird's nest, making a slight indentation in the center of each one.
3. Cool completely and decorate by placing candies in the center of each nest.

ALMOND BUTTERCRUNCH CANDY
Servings: 56 | Prep: 10m | Cooks: 20m | Total: 2h30m

NUTRITION FACTS

Calories: 162 | Carbohydrates: 15.2g | Fat: 11.4g | Protein: 1.2g | Cholesterol: 21mg

INGREDIENTS

- 2 (11.5 ounce) packages milk chocolate chips, divided
- 1 pound brown sugar
- 2 cups butter
- 1 cup blanched slivered almonds, divided

DIRECTIONS

1. Preheat oven to 200 degrees F (95 degrees C). Grease a 14 x 18 inch cookie sheet.
2. Sprinkle one package of chocolate chips on prepared pan. Place in warm oven until chips melt, about 5 minutes. Remove from oven, and spread melted chocolate over bottom of pan; set aside.
3. In a large heavy saucepan over medium-high heat, combine butter and brown sugar. Stirring constantly, heat to 300 to 310 degrees F (149 to 154 degrees C), or until a small amount of syrup dropped into cold water forms hard, brittle threads. Immediately remove from heat. Stir in 3/4 cup slivered almonds and pour onto pan with melted chocolate; spread mixture evenly.
4. Sprinkle remaining package of chocolate chips over the almond layer. The heat from the almond layer will melt the chocolate chips; spread melted chocolate evenly. Sprinkle remaining 1/4 cup almonds over chocolate.
5. Cut into squares, or allow to harden in a solid sheet and break it apart like brittle. Cool completely before removing from pan.

BRANDY OR RUM BALLS

Servings: 60 | Prep: 25m | Cooks: 15m | Total: 40m

NUTRITION FACTS

Calories: 92 | Carbohydrates: 9.9g | Fat: 5.1g | Protein: 1.2g | Cholesterol: <1mg

INGREDIENTS

- 1 (5 ounce) can evaporated milk
- 1 (16 ounce) package vanilla wafers, crushed very fine
- 1 cup semisweet chocolate chips
- 2 cups finely chopped walnuts
- 1/2 cup brandy
- 1 cup confectioners' sugar for rolling

DIRECTIONS

1. In the microwave or in a metal bowl over a pan of simmering water, melt evaporated milk and chocolate chips, stirring frequently until smooth. Remove from heat and stir in the crushed vanilla wafers and brandy until well blended. Roll the dough into small balls and roll the balls in chopped walnuts, then in confectioners' sugar. Store covered in the refrigerator.

ELISA'S FAMOUS FUDGE

Servings: 48 | Prep: 20m | Cooks: 10m | Total: 2h30m

NUTRITION FACTS

Calories: 82 | Carbohydrates: 13.4g | Fat: 3.1g | Protein: 0.5g | Cholesterol: 2mg

INGREDIENTS

- 1 1/2 cups white sugar
- 3/4 cup semisweet chocolate chips
- 2/3 cup evaporated milk
- 3/4 cup butterscotch chips
- 2 tablespoons butter
- 1/2 cup chopped pecans
- 1/4 teaspoon salt
- 1 teaspoon vanilla extract
- 1 (7 ounce) jar marshmallow creme

DIRECTIONS

1. Line an 8-inch square dish with foil.
2. In a heavy saucepan over medium heat, combine sugar, evaporated milk, butter and salt. Bring to a boil and let roll 5 minutes. Remove from heat and stir in marshmallow creme, chocolate chips, butterscotch chips, pecans and vanilla. Continue stirring until marshmallow creme is melted and all ingredients are thoroughly combined. Pour into prepared dish.
3. Refrigerate for 2 hours, until firm. Lift from dish, remove foil, and cut into pieces.

OLD-FASHIONED PEANUT BRITTLE
Servings: 20 | Prep: 15m | Cooks: 15m | Total: 1h15m

NUTRITION FACTS

Calories: 143 | Carbohydrates: 23.1g | Fat: 5.4g | Protein: 2.8g | Cholesterol: 0mg

INGREDIENTS

- 1 1/2 cups white sugar
- 1 1/2 cups raw peanuts
- 1/2 cup white corn syrup
- 1/2 teaspoon salt
- 1/4 cup water
- 1 1/2 teaspoons baking soda

DIRECTIONS

1. Spray two cookie sheets with non-stick spray coating.
2. In a 4 quart saucepan over medium-high heat, combine the sugar, corn syrup and water. Heat to boiling and add peanuts. Cook until peanuts become golden in color and syrup mixture beads off nuts when raised out of pan. Quickly mix in the salt and baking soda until well blended.
3. Pour the mixture onto the prepared cookie sheets. Allow mixture to spread on it's own. Cool completely, and break into pieces. Store in air-tight container or plastic bag.

TEXAS PRALINES
Servings: 56 | Prep: 10m | Cooks: 20m | Total: 30m

NUTRITION FACTS

Calories: 255 | Carbohydrates: 18.5g | Fat: 20.8g | Protein: 1.7g | Cholesterol: 29mg

INGREDIENTS

- nonstick cooking spray
- 2 cups heavy cream
- 2 cups white sugar
- 2 teaspoons vanilla extract

- 2 cups light corn syrup
- 8 cups pecans
- 1 pound butter

DIRECTIONS

1. Line 2 baking sheets with aluminum foil. Coat with nonstick cooking spray.
2. In a large saucepan over medium heat, combine sugar and corn syrup. Heat to 250 degrees F (120 degrees C). Remove from heat, and stir in butter until melted. Gradually stir in cream. Return to heat. Cook, stirring constantly, until temperature reaches 242 degrees F (116 degrees C). Remove from heat, and stir in vanilla and pecans.
3. Drop by spoonful onto prepared pans. Cool completely, then wrap with plastic.

PRETZEL SMOOCHIES
Servings: 20 | Prep: 10m | Cooks: 5m | Total: 45m

NUTRITION FACTS

Calories: 85 | Carbohydrates: 15.2g | Fat: 2.1g | Protein: 1.7g | Cholesterol: 1mg

INGREDIENTS

- 20 mini pretzels
- 20 foil-wrapped milk chocolate pieces (such as Hershey's Kisses
- 20 candy-coated milk chocolate pieces (such as M&M's)

DIRECTIONS

1. Preheat oven to 350 degrees F (175 degrees C).
2. Place pretzels on a baking sheet lined with aluminum foil.
3. Place an unwrapped chocolate piece onto each pretzel.
4. Heat the pretzels and chocolate candies in the preheated oven until the milk chocolate pieces become soft but hold their shape, 30 seconds to 1 minute. Watch carefully and don't let the chocolate melt to the point of dripping.
5. Remove the pretzels from the oven and allow to stand for 1 minute to allow candy to finish softening.
6. Push a colored candy-coated piece into the center of each chocolate kiss, pushing it down and flattening it. Set treats aside to cool to room temperature and fully set, about 30 minutes.

CARAMEL POPCORN WITH MARSHMALLOW
Servings: 8 | Prep: 5m | Cooks: 15m | Total: 20m

NUTRITION FACTS

Calories: 562 | Carbohydrates: 74.5g | Fat: 30g | Protein: 2.9g | Cholesterol: 61mg

INGREDIENTS

- 23 large marshmallows
- 1 cup butter
- 2 cups brown sugar
- 1 teaspoon vanilla extract
- 1/4 cup light corn syrup (such as Karo)
- 2 (3.5 ounce) packages microwave popcorn, popped

DIRECTIONS

1. Cook and stir the marshmallows, brown sugar, corn syrup, butter, and vanilla extract together in a pot over medium-low heat until the marshmallows are completely melted, 5 to 7 minutes.
2. Put the popcorn in a large bowl; pour the marshmallow mixture over the popcorn and gently stir with a big spoon to coat.

CARAMEL CORN TREAT BAGS
Servings: 8 | Prep: 15m | Cooks: 45m | Total: 1h

NUTRITION FACTS

Calories: 459 | Carbohydrates: 67.8g | Fat: 21g | Protein: 1.7g | Cholesterol: 31mg

INGREDIENTS

- 4 quarts popped popcorn
- 1/2 teaspoon salt
- 1 cup brown sugar
- 1/2 teaspoon baking soda
- 1/2 cup Karo Light or Dark Corn Syrup
- 1 teaspoon Spice Islands Pure Vanilla Extract
- 1/2 cup butter or margarine
- Halloween candies, nuts, dried fruits, etc.

DIRECTIONS

1. Spray a large shallow roasting pan with cooking spray. Add popcorn and place in preheated 250 degrees F oven while preparing caramel.
2. Mix brown sugar, corn syrup, butter and salt in a heavy 2-quart saucepan. Stirring constantly, bring to a boil over medium heat.
3. Boil 5 minutes WITHOUT STIRRING. Remove from heat. Stir in baking soda and vanilla.
4. Pour syrup mixture over warm popcorn, stirring to coat evenly.
5. Bake for 45 minutes, stirring occasionally. Remove from oven and spread on foil that has been sprayed with cooking spray. Cool; break apart. Store in tightly covered container.

6. To serve, set out small bowls of your favorite candies, nuts or fruits and let your guests individualize their own Halloween treat.

GRAMMA'S EASY PEANUT BUTTER FUDGE
Servings: 24 | Prep: 20m | Cooks: 20m | Total: 40m

NUTRITION FACTS

Calories: 263 | Carbohydrates: 40.9g | Fat: 10.3g | Protein: 4.6g | Cholesterol: 1mg

INGREDIENTS

- 1 1/3 cups milk
- 1 1/2 cups peanut butter
- 2 pounds brown sugar
- 1 teaspoon vanilla extract
- 1/4 cup margarine

DIRECTIONS

1. In a medium saucepan over medium heat, combine milk and sugar. Heat to between 234 and 240 degrees F (112 to 116 degrees C), or until a small amount of syrup dropped into cold water forms a soft ball that flattens when removed from the water and placed on a flat surface.
2. Remove from the heat and stir in margarine, peanut butter and vanilla. Quickly spread into a 9x13 inch dish. Allow to cool almost completely before cutting into squares. Store in an airtight container.

CHOCOLATE ALMOND BARK
Servings: 16 | Prep: 5m | Cooks: 10m | Total: 45m

NUTRITION FACTS

Calories: 130 | Carbohydrates: 14.2g | Fat: 8.4g | Protein: 2.1g | Cholesterol: 5mg

INGREDIENTS

- 1/2 cup chopped almonds
- 2 cups milk chocolate chips
- 1 tablespoon shortening

DIRECTIONS

1. Line a 9x13 inch baking pan with parchment paper. Set aside. Put chopped almonds In a skillet. Cook, stirring often over medium high heat, until golden brown. Remove from heat.

2. In a metal bowl over a pan of simmering water, melt chocolate chips and shortening until smooth. Remove from heat and stir in 1/2 the toasted almonds. Spread onto the prepared baking pan. Sprinkle with remaining almonds, and chill 30 minutes, or until solid. Break into bite-size pieces to serve.

FUDGE BONBONS

Servings: 60 | Prep: 19m | Cooks: 6m | Total: 25m

NUTRITION FACTS

Calories: 94 | Carbohydrates: 13.1g | Fat: 4.5g | Protein: 1.5g | Cholesterol: 5mg

INGREDIENTS

- 2 cups semisweet chocolate chips
- 2 cups all-purpose flour
- 1/4 cup butter
- 1 teaspoon vanilla extract
- 1 (14 ounce) can sweetened condensed milk
- 60 milk chocolate candy kisses, unwrapped

DIRECTIONS

1. Preheat oven to 350 degrees F (175 degrees C). In a heavy saucepan over low heat, stir chocolate chips and butter until melted and smooth. Stir in condensed milk, flour and vanilla until well blended.
2. Shape one level teaspoon of chocolate chip dough around each candy kiss. Arrange bonbons one inch apart on ungreased cookie sheets.
3. Bake 6 minutes. Bonbons will be soft and shiny, but will firm up as they cool.

CARAMEL FOR APPLES

Servings: 12 | Prep: 5m | Cooks: 20m | Total: 40m

NUTRITION FACTS

Calories: 380 | Carbohydrates: 47.1g | Fat: 22.3g | Protein: 0.9g | Cholesterol: 75mg

INGREDIENTS

- 1 1/2 cups white sugar
- 2 cups heavy cream
- 1 cup light corn syrup
- 1/2 cup butter at room temperature
- 1 teaspoon salt
- 1 teaspoon vanilla extract

DIRECTIONS

1. In a large heavy saucepan, combine the white sugar, corn syrup, and salt. Bring to a boil and heat to between 234 and 240 degrees F (112 to 116 degrees C), or until a small amount of syrup dropped into cold water forms a soft ball that flattens when removed from the water and placed on a flat surface.
2. Stir in the butter and heavy cream carefully - the mixture will bubble up. Remove from the heat and stir in the vanilla. Cool slightly before dipping apples or other fruit; caramel should cling to a spoon and drip slowly. Let apples set on waxed paper or parchment.

MORGAN'S AMAZING PEPPERMINT BARK
Servings: 15 | Prep: 15m | Cooks: 1m | Total: 1h15m

NUTRITION FACTS

Calories: 83 | Carbohydrates: 12.2g | Fat: 3.6g | Protein: 0.7g | Cholesterol: 2mg

INGREDIENTS

- 1 (6 ounce) package white chocolate, chopped
- 3 peppermint candy canes

DIRECTIONS

1. Line a baking sheet with waxed paper.
2. Place white chocolate in a microwave-safe bowl; heat in the microwave until melted, 60 to 90 seconds. Stir until smooth.
3. Place one gallon-sized resealable bag inside a second gallon-sized bag, creating a double-layered bag. Place candy canes inside the inner bag and seal. Crush the candy canes inside bag with a rolling pin. Stir crushed candy canes into melted white chocolate.
4. Pour white chocolate mixture onto the prepared baking sheet. Chill in refrigerator until hardened, 1 hour.

CHERRIES AND CHOCOLATE FUDGE
Servings: 60 | Prep: 10m | Cooks: 3m | Total: 2h13m

NUTRITION FACTS

Calories: 61 | Carbohydrates: 8.6g | Fat: 3g | Protein: 1g | Cholesterol: 2mg

INGREDIENTS

- 1 (14 ounce) can sweetened condensed milk
- 1 teaspoon almond extract
- 1 (12 ounce) package semisweet chocolate chips

- 1/4 cup pecan halves
- 1/2 cup chopped almonds
- 1/4 cup candied cherries, halved
- 1/2 cup chopped candied cherries

DIRECTIONS

1. Line an 8 x 8 inch square pan with aluminum foil.
2. In a microwave-safe bowl combine sweetened condensed milk and chocolate chips; microwave on high for 1 1/2 minutes, or until chocolate is melted. Stir until smooth. Stir in chopped almonds, chopped cherries and almond extract. Pour into prepared pan and spread evenly. Place pecan halves and cherry halves on top.
3. Cover and refrigerate for 2 hours, or until firm. Cut into 1 inch squares. Store, covered, in refrigerator.

NEVER-FAIL FUDGE
Servings: 12 | Prep: 15m | Cooks: 15m | Total: 45m

NUTRITION FACTS

Calories: 283 | Carbohydrates: 43.4g | Fat: 12.9g | Protein: 1.8g | Cholesterol: 16mg

INGREDIENTS

- 4 cups confectioners' sugar
- 1 tablespoon vanilla extract
- 1/2 cup unsweetened cocoa powder
- 1/4 teaspoon salt
- 6 tablespoons butter
- 1 cup chopped pecans
- 1/4 cup milk

DIRECTIONS

1. Butter a 9x9 inch dish.
2. Combine sugar, cocoa, butter, milk, vanilla and salt in the top of a double boiler over simmering water. Cook, stirring, until smooth. Remove from heat and beat until mixture loses its gloss. Stir in chopped nuts and pour quickly into prepared pan.
3. Let cool completely before cutting into squares.

CHOCOLATE PEANUT BUTTER CHIP FUDGE
Servings: 28 | Prep: 15m | Cooks: 2h | Total: 2h15m

NUTRITION FACTS

Calories: 171 | Carbohydrates: 16.3g | Fat: 7.5g | Protein: 2.9g | Cholesterol: 5mg

INGREDIENTS

- 2 cups semi-sweet chocolate chips
- 1 teaspoon vanilla extract
- 1 (14 ounce) can EAGLE BRAND Sweetened Condensed Milk
- 1 cup peanut butter chips

DIRECTIONS

1. In heavy saucepan, over low heat, melt chocolate chips with EAGLE BRAND(R) and vanilla, stirring frequently.
2. Remove from heat. Add peanut butter chips; stir just to distribute chips throughout mixture.
3. Spread evenly into wax paper lined 8- or 9-inch square pan. Chill 2 hours or until firm. Turn fudge onto cutting board; peel off paper and cut into squares. Store leftovers covered in refrigerator.

WHITE CHOCOLATE GRAPES
Servings: 20 | Prep: 20m | Cooks: 2m | Total: 22m

NUTRITION FACTS

Calories: 163 | Carbohydrates: 15.7g | Fat: 10.5g | Protein: 3.1g | Cholesterol: 4mg

INGREDIENTS

- 2 cups white chocolate chips
- 1 pound seedless grapes
- 2 teaspoons shortening
- 1 cup finely chopped salted peanuts

DIRECTIONS

1. Combine the white chocolate chips and shortening in a small microwave-safe bowl. Heat in the microwave for 30 second intervals, stirring between each, until melted and smooth. Spread the chopped peanuts out on a piece of waxed paper or a dinner plate.
2. Dip clean, dry grapes into the chocolate, then roll in the peanuts. Set on waxed paper until dry. Warm chocolate as needed in the microwave to keep it liquid.

CHINESE NEW YEAR CHOCOLATE CANDY
Servings: 24 | Prep: 5m | Cooks: 30m | Total: 1h

NUTRITION FACTS

Calories: 276 | Carbohydrates: 25.5g | Fat: 18.1g | Protein: 4.8g | Cholesterol: 0mg

INGREDIENTS

- 2 cups semisweet chocolate chips
- 2 1/2 cups dry-roasted peanuts
- 2 cups butterscotch chips
- 4 cups chow mein noodles

DIRECTIONS

1. Butter a 9x13 inch dish.
2. Melt chocolate and butterscotch chips in the top of a double boiler over simmering water. Remove from heat and stir in peanuts. Stir in noodles until all is well coated. Press into prepared dish. Chill until set; cut into squares.

HOMEMADE MARSHMALLOWS
Servings: 20 | Prep: 10m | Cooks: 20m | Total: 8h30m

NUTRITION FACTS

Calories: 80 | Carbohydrates: 20g | Fat: 0g | Protein: 0.6g | Cholesterol: 0mg

INGREDIENTS

- 2 envelopes unflavored gelatin
- 2 cups white sugar
- 1 1/4 cups water, divided

DIRECTIONS

1. In a large mixing bowl, stir together gelatin and 1/2 cup plus 2 tablespoons water. Set aside to soften.
2. Combine remaining 1/2 cup plus 2 tablespoons of water and sugar in a saucepan. Bring to a boil, stirring occasionally to dissolve the sugar. Do not stir once the sugar syrup begins to boil. Heat to 270 degrees F (130 degrees C).
3. With an electric mixer running on low speed, carefully pour hot sugar syrup into gelatin mixture. Beat on high speed until mixture is light and fluffy and mixture is no longer warm to the touch, 10 to 15 minutes. Pour into a lightly greased 9x13 inch baking dish and let set 8 hours or overnight. Cut into squares and serve.

CANDIED CITRUS PEEL
Servings: 4 | Prep: 15m | Cooks: 45m | Total: 9h

NUTRITION FACTS

Calories: 121 | Carbohydrates: 31.3g | Fat: 0.1g | Protein: 0.4g | Cholesterol: 0mg

INGREDIENTS

- 1 cup orange peel, cut into strips
- 1/2 cup white sugar
- 1/4 cup water

DIRECTIONS

1. Place peel strips in large saucepan and cover with water. Bring to a boil over high heat, then reduce heat and simmer 10 minutes longer. Drain. Repeat this process two more times.
2. In a medium saucepan, heat sugar and 1/4 cup water over high heat until boiling. Place peel in sugar mixture, reduce heat and simmer 15 minutes, until sugar is dissolved. Remove peel with slotted spoon and dry on wire rack overnight. Store in airtight container.

CREAMY ORANGE FUDGE

Servings: 12 | Prep: 10m | Cooks: 10m | Total: 20m

NUTRITION FACTS

Calories: 785 | Carbohydrates: 108.3g | Fat: 37.4g | Protein: 7.3g | Cholesterol: 57mg

INGREDIENTS

- 2 pounds white chocolate, melted
- 6 cups confectioners' sugar
- 2 (8 ounce) packages cream cheese
- 1 tablespoon orange extract

DIRECTIONS

1. Beat cream cheese into melted chocolate until well blended. Beat in confectioner's sugar until mixture is smooth. Stir in orange extract. Spread in an 8x8 inch dish and let set before cutting into squares. Store in refrigerator.

MARIAN'S FUDGE

Servings: 20 | Prep: 10m | Cooks: 30m | Total: 1h10m

NUTRITION FACTS

Calories: 103 | Carbohydrates: 21.4g | Fat: 2.3g | Protein: 0.8g | Cholesterol: 3mg

INGREDIENTS

- 2 (1 ounce) squares unsweetened baking chocolate
- 2 cups white sugar

- 1 tablespoon butter
- 1 pinch salt
- 1 cup milk
- 1 teaspoon vanilla extract

DIRECTIONS

1. Butter a 9x9 inch dish.
2. In a medium saucepan over medium heat, combine chocolate, butter and milk. Bring to a boil and let boil 1 minute. Stir in sugar and salt until dissolved. Heat, stirring constantly, to between 234 and 240 degrees F (112 to 116 degrees C), or until a small amount of syrup dropped into cold water forms a soft ball that flattens when removed from the water and placed on a flat surface. Remove from heat and stir in vanilla. Let cool 10 minutes.
3. Beat fudge with a spoon until it loses its gloss. Pour quickly into the buttered dish. Refrigerate 30 minutes, until firm.

SUCRE A LA CREME

Servings: 25 | Prep: 5m | Cooks: 10m | Total: 15m

NUTRITION FACTS

Calories: 97 | Carbohydrates: 16.9g | Fat: 3.5g | Protein: 0.2g | Cholesterol: 13mg

INGREDIENTS

- 1 cup white sugar
- 1 cup brown sugar
- 1 cup heavy cream

DIRECTIONS

1. In a large microwave-safe bowl, stir together the white sugar, brown sugar and cream. Cook at full power for 10 minutes, stirring twice. Let stand for 5 minutes.
2. Use an electric mixer on low speed to beat the mixture for 4 minutes. Pour into a buttered 8 inch square glass baking dish. Refrigerate for 1 hour or until firm. Cut into squares when set.

EASTER BIRD'S NESTS

Servings: 10 | Prep: 15m | Cooks: 5m | Total: 20m

NUTRITION FACTS

Calories: 365 | Carbohydrates: 40.2g | Fat: 21.1g | Protein: 4.6g | Cholesterol: 17mg

INGREDIENTS

- 3 cups miniature marshmallows
- 4 cups crispy chow mein noodles
- 1/4 cup creamy peanut butter
- cooking spray
- 3 tablespoons butter
- 40 candy-coated milk chocolate eggs

DIRECTIONS

1. Cook and stir marshmallows, peanut butter, and butter in a saucepan over medium heat until the marshmallows melt completely into the mixture, about 5 minutes.
2. Put chow mein noodles into a large bowl. Pour marshmallow mixture over the chow mein noodles; stir to coat.
3. Spray hands with cooking spray or coat with butter so the noodles will not stick to your hands. Scoop noodle mixture from bowl with an ice cream scoop and form into balls, hollowing the center out to create the nest. Arrange 4 chocolate eggs into each nest.

INGREDIENT PEANUT BUTTER FUDGE
Servings: 48 | Prep: 10m | Cooks: 10m | Total: 1h20m

NUTRITION FACTS

Calories: 114 | Carbohydrates: 7.7g | Fat: 8.4g | Protein: 3.2g | Cholesterol: 2mg

INGREDIENTS

- 1 pound white confectioners' coating (white almond bark), broken up
- 1 (18 ounce) jar peanut butter (such as Jif)

DIRECTIONS

1. Line an 8x8-inch baking dish with plastic wrap long enough to overhang the dish by several inches on each side.
2. Place broken coating into a large glass microwave-safe bowl and melt on low power in microwave oven, about 5 minutes, stirring after every 30 seconds to 1 minute. When coating is smooth and creamy, stir peanut butter into coating until fudge is thoroughly combined. Spread fudge into the prepared baking dish.
3. Refrigerate fudge until set, 1 to 2 hours. Lift fudge out of the pan using the plastic wrap for handles and slice into squares with a pizza cutter.

PEANUT BUTTER BON-BONS
Servings: 100 | Prep: 10m | Cooks: 20m | Total: 30m

NUTRITION FACTS

Calories: 75 | Carbohydrates: 8.1g | Fat: 4.5g | Protein: 1.5g | Cholesterol: 4mg

INGREDIENTS

- 2 cups peanut butter
- 3 cups crispy rice cereal
- 3/4 cup butter
- 6 (1 ounce) squares semisweet chocolate, chopped
- 4 1/2 cups confectioners' sugar

DIRECTIONS

1. In a medium saucepan, melt together the peanut butter and butter, stirring occasionally until warm and smooth. In a large bowl, stir together the confectioners' sugar and rice cereal; pour the peanut butter mixture over the cereal mixture and use your hands to blend well. Roll tablespoonfuls of the mixture into balls and chill.
2. In the microwave or in a metal bowl over a pan of simmering water, melt chocolate chips, stirring frequently until smooth. Dip the peanut butter balls into the chocolate using a toothpick. Place onto waxed paper to set.

STATE FAIR KETTLE CORN
Servings: 4 | Prep: 5m | Cooks: 10m | Total: 1h

NUTRITION FACTS

Calories: 199 | Carbohydrates: 17.2g | Fat: 14.4g | Protein: 1.5g | Cholesterol: 0mg

INGREDIENTS

- 1/4 cup corn oil
- 1 1/2 teaspoons brown sugar
- 1/4 cup unpopped popcorn
- salt to taste
- 2 tablespoons white sugar

DIRECTIONS

1. Heat the corn oil in a large pot over medium heat. Stir in the corn kernels once hot. When the first couple of kernels pop, stir in the white and brown sugars. Cover the pot with a lid, and agitate the pot in a circular motion on the stove. Allow the corn to pop, agitating constantly, until the rate has slowed down to one pop every two or three seconds. Remove the pot from the stove, and shake the pot until the popping stops. Pour into a large bowl, and allow to cool to room temperature. Break apart the large clumps of popcorn by hand, and season with salt to taste.

CHERRY-PISTACHIO BARK

Servings: 150 | Prep: 15m | Cooks: 7m | Total: 1h22m

NUTRITION FACTS

Calories: 45 | Carbohydrates: 4.8g | Fat: 2.6g | Protein: 0.7g | Cholesterol: 1mg

INGREDIENTS

- 1 1/4 cups dried cherries
- 4 (3 ounce) bars vanilla-flavored candy coating
- 2 tablespoons water
- 1 1/4 cups chopped pistachio nuts
- 2 (11 ounce) packages white chocolate chips

DIRECTIONS

1. In a small glass bowl, microwave cherries with water on high for 2 minutes; drain, and set aside.
2. In a separate microwave-safe bowl, microwave chocolate chips and candy coating together until melted and smooth, stirring occasionally. Stir in cherries and chopped pistachios, and spread into a wax paper-lined 15x10 inch pan. Chill for 1 hour, or until firm.
3. Cut into 1 inch squares, and enjoy. Store unused portion in an air-tight container.

TOLL HOUSE FAMOUS FUDGE

Servings: 6 | Prep: m | Cooks: m | Total: m

NUTRITION FACTS

Calories: 74 | Carbohydrates: 11.7g | Fat: 3g | Protein: 0.7g | Cholesterol: 2mg

INGREDIENTS

- 1 1/2 cups granulated sugar
- 2 cups miniature marshmallows
- 2/3 cup NESTLE CARNATION Evaporated Milk
- 1 1/2 cups NESTLE TOLL HOUSE Semi-Sweet Chocolate Morsels
- 2 tablespoons butter or margarine
- 1/2 cup chopped pecans (optional)
- 1/4 teaspoon salt
- 1 teaspoon vanilla extract

DIRECTIONS

1. LINE 8-inch-square baking pan with foil.

2. COMBINE sugar, evaporated milk, butter and salt in medium, heavy-duty saucepan. Bring to a full rolling boil over medium heat, stirring constantly. Boil, stirring constantly, for 4 to 5 minutes. Remove from heat.
3. STIR in marshmallows, morsels, nuts and vanilla extract. Stir vigorously for 1 minute or until marshmallows are melted. Pour into prepared baking pan; refrigerate for 2 hours or until firm. Lift from pan; remove foil. Cut into pieces.

COCONUT ICE
Servings: 20 | Prep: 5m | Cooks: 30m | Total: 1h30m

NUTRITION FACTS

Calories: 119 | Carbohydrates: 21.5g | Fat: 4g | Protein: 0.4g | Cholesterol: 0mg

INGREDIENTS

- 2 cups white sugar
- 1 1/3 cups flaked coconut
- 2/3 cup water
- 2 drops red food coloring
- 1 teaspoon vanilla extract

DIRECTIONS

1. Line a 7 x 7 inch pan with parchment or waxed paper. In a medium, heavy-bottomed saucepan, heat sugar and water gently, without boiling, until sugar has dissolved. Then, bring to a boil and cook until it reaches 240 degrees F/120 degrees C on a candy thermometer, or a little syrup dropped in a glass of cold water forms a soft ball.
2. Remove from heat and immediately stir in vanilla and coconut. Continue stirring until mixture begins to thicken, 5 to 10 minutes.
3. Pour half of the mixture into the prepared pan and level the surface with a knife or spatula. Tint the other half of the mixture by stirring in the food coloring. Pour the pink mixture on top of other layer, and level the surface. Press all down firmly with the back of a spoon and allow to harden. When firm, turn out of the pan, remove the paper and cut into squares with a sharp knife.

WALNUT MAPLE FUDGE
Servings: 50 | Prep: 20m | Cooks: 10m | Total: 8h

NUTRITION FACTS

Calories: 144 | Carbohydrates: 17.7g | Fat: 7.7g | Protein: 1.8g | Cholesterol: 6mg

INGREDIENTS

- 2 cups white sugar
- 3 cups white chocolate chips

- 1 cup evaporated milk
- 1 cup chopped walnuts
- 3 tablespoons butter
- 2 1/2 teaspoons maple flavored extract
- 3 cups miniature marshmallows
- 50 walnut halves

DIRECTIONS

1. In a medium saucepan over medium heat, combine sugar, evaporated milk and butter. Bring to a boil and let roll 5 minutes. Remove from heat and quickly stir in marshmallows, white chocolate, chopped walnuts and maple flavoring. Spread in a 9x13 inch dish. Top with large walnut pieces, evenly spaced. Chill 8 hours or overnight. To serve, cut around large walnuts.

EASY CASHEW SEA SALT TOFFEE
Servings: 8 | Prep: 5m | Cooks: 8m | Total: 1h

NUTRITION FACTS

Calories: 356 | Carbohydrates: 38.7g | Fat: 22.7g | Protein: 3.1g | Cholesterol: 36mg

INGREDIENTS

- 1/2 cup butter or margarine
- 1 cup sugar
- 1 1/4 teaspoons Diamond Crystal Sea Salt, divided
- 1/4 cup water
- 3/4 cup coarsely chopped cashews, divided
- 3/4 cup milk chocolate chips or chopped milk chocolate

DIRECTIONS

1. Butter the top edges of a 2-quart microwave-safe casserole. Add butter, 1 teaspoon of the Diamond Crystal(R) Sea Salt, sugar, and water to the casserole. DO NOT STIR. Microwave on high for 6 to 8 minutes. Check contents for color change. Continue microwaving on high a minute at a time until the mixture just begins to turn a tan color. You need to watch it carefully, and remember: DON'T STIR.
2. Sprinkle 1/2 cup of the chopped cashews into a 9-into circle on a Silpat mat, parchment paper, or on a buttered baking sheet.
3. Carefully pour the liquid mixture evenly over the top of the cashews. Immediately sprinkle on the chocolate chips. Allow to sit for 1 minute to melt the chocolate.
4. Use spatula to smooth out chocolate over the entire sheet of candy.

5. Sprinkle the remaining cashews and 1/4 teaspoon Diamond Crystal(R) Sea Salt over the top. Refrigerate to cool completely. When cool, break into bite-sized pieces. Store tightly covered in refrigerator.

CHEF JOHN'S CHRISTMAS MIRACLE FUDGE
Servings: 24 | Prep: 15m | Cooks: 5m | Total: 50m

NUTRITION FACTS

Calories: 78 | Carbohydrates: 5.8g | Fat: 6.5g | Protein: 0.7g | Cholesterol: 0mg

INGREDIENTS

- 1/2 cup good-quality unsweetened cocoa (such as Guittard Cocoa Rouge), not packe
- 1/2 cup real maple syrup
- 1 teaspoon vanilla extract
- 1 pinch salt
- 1/2 cup refined coconut oil, melted
- 1/2 cup chopped walnuts
- 1 teaspoon unsweetened cocoa powder for dusting, or as neede

DIRECTIONS

1. Place 1/2 cup cocoa powder into a mixing bowl and stir in maple syrup, vanilla extract, and salt. Pour in melted coconut oil and stir until thoroughly combined. Continue to stir until coconut oil hardens and the mixture looks grainy and thick.
2. Place walnuts into a dry skillet over medium heat; shake skillet until walnuts are hot and smell nutty and fragrant, 30 seconds to 1 minute. Turn off heat and let walnuts cool slightly, about 1 more minute.
3. Stir warm walnuts into fudge; mixture will soften from the walnuts' heat. Stir fudge until smooth and glossy.
4. Pour fudge into a silicone mold for making small ice cubes. Scrape any excess fudge back into the mixing bowl. Smooth the tops of the fudge pieces.
5. Wrap mold in plastic wrap and freeze until fudge is firm and set, at least 30 minutes. Remove plastic wrap and pop each fudge piece out of the mold. Dust pieces lightly with 1 teaspoon cocoa powder before serving or packaging as gifts. Serve cold; freeze leftovers.

BUTTERSCOTCH CANDY
Servings: 40 | Prep: 10m | Cooks: 15m | Total: 45m

NUTRITION FACTS

Calories: 30 | Carbohydrates: 5.2g | Fat: 1.2g | Protein: 0g | Cholesterol: 3mg

INGREDIENTS

- 1/2 cup brown sugar
- 1/2 cup white sugar
- 1/4 cup butte
- 2 teaspoons vinegar
- 1/2 cup water
- 1 pinch salt
- 1/2 teaspoon vanilla extract

DIRECTIONS

1. Generously butter a 10x15 inch baking pan (with sides).
2. In a medium saucepan over medium heat, combine brown sugar, butter, white sugar, water, vinegar and salt. Cover and bring to a boil. Remove lid and heat, without stirring, to 270 to 290 degrees F (132 to 143 degrees C), or until a small amount of syrup dropped into cold water forms hard but pliable threads. Pour in vanilla, but do not stir. Remove from heat and pour into prepared pan. Let cool slightly before cutting into squares and allowing candy to cool completely.

DELICIOUS MATZO CANDY
Servings: 48 | Prep: 15m | Cooks: 15m | Total: 55m

NUTRITION FACTS

Calories: 128 | Carbohydrates: 15.2g | Fat: 7.5g | Protein: 1.5g | Cholesterol: 10mg

INGREDIENTS

- 12 matzo crackers
- 1 cup butter
- 1 cup brown suga
- 1 (12 ounce) bag semisweet chocolate chips
- 1 cup chopped walnuts

DIRECTIONS

1. Preheat an oven to 350 degrees F (175 degrees C). Line two baking sheets with aluminum foil. Place the matzo crackers in a single layer on the lined baking sheets, breaking to fit, if necessary.

2. Bring the butter and brown sugar to a boil in a heavy bottomed saucepan over medium heat. Continue to cook, stirring constantly, until thick and smooth, about 3 minutes. Pour the hot sugar mixture over the matzo, and spread evenly with a heat proof spatula.

3. Place the caramel topped matzo in the preheated oven for 10 minutes. Remove from oven and evenly sprinkle the chocolate chips on top. Return pans to oven to melt chocolate, about 1 minute. Smooth melted chocolate to completely cover the caramel. Sprinkle with the chopped walnuts. Chill in refrigerator for 20 minutes, or until set. Break into small pieces to serve.

CHOCOLATE COVERED POTATO CHIPS
Servings: 16 | Prep: 30m | Cooks: 0m | Total: 30m

NUTRITION FACTS

Calories: 363 | Carbohydrates: 35.4g | Fat: 21.6g | Protein: 4.8g | Cholesterol: 7mg

INGREDIENTS

- 1 pound high quality milk chocolate, chopped
- 8 cups ridged potato chips

DIRECTIONS

1. Place about 3/4 of the chocolate into a heat safe bowl, and place over the top of a pan of simmering water. If you have a double boiler, use that. Heat, stirring occasionally until the chocolate has melted, then continue to heat the chocolate to 110 degrees F (43 degrees C), stirring occasionally. You may use a meat thermometer if your candy thermometer does not go that low.

2. As soon as the melted chocolate reaches temperature, remove it from the heat, and stir in the remaining chopped chocolate until melted. Continue stirring until the chocolate has cooled to 90 degrees F (32 degrees C). Touching a dab of chocolate to your lip will feel cool.

3. Use tongs to dip potato chips one at a time into the chocolate. Place on waxed paper starting at the point farthest from you and working your way in so as not to drip on your finished chips. Cool until set. You may refrigerate if you like.

A PEANUTTY S'MORE
Servings: 1 | Prep: 1m | Cooks: 4m | Total: 5m

NUTRITION FACTS

Calories: 252 | Carbohydrates: 42.6g | Fat: 8g | Protein: 3.9g | Cholesterol: 1mg

INGREDIENTS

- 2 large marshmallows
- 2 graham cracker squares
- 1 peanut butter cup

DIRECTIONS

1. Cook the marshmallows over an open flame or hot coals until they are browned outside, and soft all the way through, 2 to 4 minutes.
2. Place the marshmallows on top of one of the graham cracker squares. Place the peanut butter cup on top of the marshmallows. Top with the last graham cracker square.

OLD FASHIONED FUDGE
Servings: 50 | Prep: 15m | Cooks: 30m | Total: 45m

NUTRITION FACTS

Calories: 41 | Carbohydrates: 9g | Fat: 0.7g | Protein: 0.3g | Cholesterol: 2mg

INGREDIENTS

- 1/2 cup unsweetened cocoa powder
- 2 cups white sugar
- 1/4 teaspoon salt
- 1 tablespoon light corn syrup
- 1 cup milk
- 1 tablespoon vanilla extract
- 2 tablespoons butter

DIRECTIONS

1. In a medium saucepan, stir together the cocoa powder, sugar and salt. Mix in corn syrup, and milk until well blended. Add butter, and heat to between 234 and 240 degrees F (112 to 116 degrees C), or until a small amount of syrup dropped into cold water forms a soft ball that flattens when removed from the water and placed on a flat surface. Stir occasionally.
2. Remove from heat, and beat with a wooden spoon until the mixture is thick and loses its gloss. Stir in vanilla, and pour into a buttered 9x9 inch baking dish. Let cool until set. Cut into small squares to serve.

GRANDMA'S TAFFY
Servings: 40 | Prep: 5m | Cooks: 15m | Total: 20m

NUTRITION FACTS

Calories: 63 | Carbohydrates: 13.5g | Fat: 1.2g | Protein: 0g | Cholesterol: 3mg

INGREDIENTS

- 2 cups sugar
- 2 tablespoons cornstarch
- 4 tablespoons butter
- 1 teaspoon salt
- 1/2 cup corn syrup
- 1 1/2 cups water
- 2 teaspoons vanilla extract
- 1 tablespoon orange, or other flavored extract
- 8 drops any color food coloring

DIRECTIONS

1. In a large saucepan, stir together the sugar and cornstarch. Add the butter, salt, corn syrup and water; mix well. Bring to a boil over medium heat, stirring to mix in butter. Heat to 275 degrees F (134 degrees C), or until a small amount of syrup dropped from a spoon forms hard but pliable threads.
2. Remove from heat, and stir in the vanilla, flavored extract and food coloring. Pour into a greased 8x8 inch baking dish. When cooled enough to handle, remove candy from the pan, and pull until it loses its shine and becomes stiff. Pull into ropes, and use scissors to cut into 1 inch pieces. Wrap each piece in waxed paper.

COCONUT BRITTLE
Servings: 25 | Prep: 5m | Cooks: 10m | Total: 1h15m

NUTRITION FACTS

Calories: 100 | Carbohydrates: 15.2g | Fat: 4.7g | Protein: 0.5g | Cholesterol: 1mg

INGREDIENTS

- 1 cup flaked coconut
- 4 ounces chopped macadamia nuts
- 1 cup white sugar
- 1 tablespoon butter
- 1/2 cup corn syrup
- 1 teaspoon vanilla extract
- 1 teaspoon baking soda

DIRECTIONS

1. Spread coconut evenly over a buttered baking sheet.
2. In a medium microwave-safe bowl, combine sugar and corn syrup. Microwave on high 3 minutes. Stir in nuts and microwave 4 minutes more. Stir in butter and vanilla and return to microwave for 1 minute. Stir in soda until light and slightly foamy. Pour over coconut in pan. Let cool until firm, 1 hour. Break into pieces.

SIMPLE MICROWAVE PEANUT BRITTLE
Servings: 32 | Prep: 10m | Cooks: 20m | Total: 30m

NUTRITION FACTS

Calories: 102 | Carbohydrates: 21.1g | Fat: 2.2g | Protein: 0.7g | Cholesterol: 2mg

INGREDIENTS

- 1 cup light corn syrup
- 2 tablespoons butter
- 2 cups white sugar
- 2 teaspoons vanilla extract
- 2/3 cup peanuts
- 2 teaspoons baking soda

DIRECTIONS

1. In a 3 quart casserole dish, combine the corn syrup, sugar and peanuts. Microwave on high for 12 minutes. Stir in butter and vanilla, cook on high for 4 minutes. Stir in baking soda.
2. Pour onto buttered cookie sheet; cool and break into pieces.

QUICK NARIYAL BURFI (INDIAN COCONUT FUDGE)
Servings: 12 | Prep: 5m | Cooks: 7m | Total: 1h12m

NUTRITION FACTS

Calories: 275 | Carbohydrates: 37.6g | Fat: 12.1g | Protein: 5.6g | Cholesterol: 17mg

INGREDIENTS

- 3 cups sweetened flaked coconut
- 1 1/2 (14 ounce) cans sweetened condensed milk
- 2/3 cup sliced almonds

- 1 tablespoon ground cardamom (optional)

DIRECTIONS

1. Grease a 9x9 inch pan. Stir together the coconut and condensed milk in a large, microwave-safe bowl. Cook on High in the microwave for 7 minutes, stirring every 30 seconds. When the coconut mixture is hot and bubbling, stir in the almonds and cardamom. Pour into the prepared pan, and smooth the top with a spatula.
2. Cool for 1 hour in the refrigerator, then cut into 1 inch squares with a greased knife.

OLD FASHIONED HARD CANDY
Servings: 16 | Prep: 5m | Cooks: 40m | Total: 45m

NUTRITION FACTS

Calories: 150 | Carbohydrates: 39.2g | Fat: 0g | Protein: 0g | Cholesterol: 0mg

INGREDIENTS

- 1/2 cup confectioners' sugar for dusting
- 1 cup water
- 2 cups white sugar
- 2/3 cup light corn syrup
- 1 teaspoon peppermint oil, or other flavored oi
- 1 teaspoon any color food coloring

DIRECTIONS

1. Generously coat a cookie sheet with confectioners' sugar, and set aside.
2. In a heavy bottomed saucepan, stir together the white sugar, water and corn syrup until sugar has dissolved. Bring to a boil over medium-high and cook to a temperature of 300 to 310 degrees F (149 to 154 degrees C), or until a small amount of syrup dropped into cold water forms hard, brittle threads. Remove from heat, and stir in the flavored oil and food coloring.
3. Immediately pour the sugar mixture onto the prepared cookie sheet in a thin stream (this helps it cool). When the candy is cool enough for the outer edge to hold its shape, cut into bite size pieces with scissors. Let cool completely, then store in an airtight container.

REINDEER POOP
Servings: 60 | Prep: 10m | Cooks: 1h30m | Total: 2h25m

NUTRITION FACTS

Calories: 174 | Carbohydrates: 13.6g | Fat: 12.8g | Protein: 4.4g | Cholesterol: 2mg

INGREDIENTS

- 1 (16 ounce) package white candy coating, coarsely choppe
- 1 (4 ounce) bar German sweet chocolate, chopped
- 1 (16 ounce) package semi-sweet chocolate chips
- 2 (16 ounce) jars dry roasted peanuts

DIRECTIONS

1. Place the white candy coating, German sweet chocolate, chocolate chips, and peanuts into a slow cooker. Set the cooker to Low, cover, and gently heat the candy for 1 1/2 hours without stirring. After 1 1/2 hours, stir the mixture, and spoon out by teaspoons onto waxed paper. Allow to cool and set, about 45 minutes.

HOMEMADE CARAMELS
Servings: 64 | Prep: 5m | Cooks: 15m | Total: 2h20m

NUTRITION FACTS

Calories: 53 | Carbohydrates: 8.7g | Fat: 2g | Protein: 0.5g | Cholesterol: 6mg

INGREDIENTS

- 1 cup light brown sugar
- 1 cup white sugar
- 1 (14 ounce) can sweetened condensed milk
- 1/2 cup butter

DIRECTIONS

1. In a medium saucepan combine brown sugar, sugar, condensed milk and butter. Heat to 250 to 265 degrees F (121 to 129 degrees C), or until a small amount of syrup dropped into cold water forms a rigid ball.
2. Pour into an 8x8 inch pan. Cool until firm and cut into squares.

PENUCHE
Servings: 64 | Prep: 10m | Cooks: 30m | Total: 40m

NUTRITION FACTS

Calories: 59 | Carbohydrates: 10.6g | Fat: 2g | Protein: 0.2g | Cholesterol: 5mg

INGREDIENTS

- 2 cups brown sugar
- 1 cup white sugar
- 1 cup heavy cream
- 2 tablespoons light corn syrup
- 1/4 teaspoon salt
- 1 teaspoon vanilla extract
- 1/2 cup chopped pecans

DIRECTIONS

1. Butter an 8x8 inch square dish.
2. In a medium saucepan over medium heat, combine brown sugar, white sugar, cream, corn syrup and salt. Stir until sugar is dissolved. Heat to between 234 and 240 degrees F (112 to 116 degrees C), or until a small amount of syrup dropped into cold water forms a soft ball that flattens when removed from the water and placed on a flat surface. Remove from heat and let cool without stirring until bottom of pan is lukewarm. Pour in vanilla and beat until creamy. Stir in nuts. Pour into prepared pan.
3. Let cool completely before cutting into squares.

RUM TRUFFLES

Servings: 24 | Prep: 10m | Cooks: 10m | Total: 1h50m

NUTRITION FACTS

Calories: 98 | Carbohydrates: 9.6g | Fat: 6.2g | Protein: 0.9g | Cholesterol: 8mg

INGREDIENTS

- 8 (1 ounce) squares bittersweet chocolate, chopped
- 1/4 cup cream
- 2 tablespoons unsalted butter
- 1/2 cup chocolate cake crumbs
- 2 teaspoons dark rum
- 1/2 cup chocolate sprinkles

DIRECTIONS

1. Line a sheet pan with aluminum foil or parchment paper. Place chopped chocolate in a heatproof bowl.

2. In a saucepan, combine cream and butter. Place over low heat, and bring to a boil. Pour over chocolate, and stir until chocolate is melted and smooth. Stir in cake crumbs and rum. Set aside until firm, but not hard.

3. Roll heaping teaspoons of chocolate mixture into balls, then roll in the chocolate sprinkles. Place on the prepared tray. Refrigerate 30 minutes or until firm. Serve in small paper cups.

MADE-IN-MINUTES NO-COOK FUDGE
Servings: 16 | Prep: 15m | Cooks: 1h | Total: 1h15m

NUTRITION FACTS

Calories: 162 | Carbohydrates: 11.6g | Fat: 14.4g | Protein: 1.1g | Cholesterol: 0mg

INGREDIENTS

- 1 cup virgin coconut oil, room temperature
- 1 cup unsweetened cocoa powder
- 1/2 cup honey

DIRECTIONS

1. Lightly grease 8x8 inch baking dish.

2. Pour the coconut oil into a bowl, and sift in the cocoa, stirring to blend evenly. Stir in the honey, and mix until smooth. Spread mixture into prepared dish, and refrigerate at least 1 hour. Cut into 1 inch squares.

CHOCOLATE COVERED BLUEBERRIES
Servings: 36 | Prep: 10m | Cooks: 5m | Total: 15m

NUTRITION FACTS

Calories: 30 | Carbohydrates: 4.1g | Fat: 1.8g | Protein: 0.3g | Cholesterol: 0mg

INGREDIENTS

- 1 cup semi-sweet chocolate chips
- 1 tablespoon shortening
- 2 cups fresh blueberries, rinsed and dried

DIRECTIONS

1. Melt chocolate in a glass bowl in the microwave, or in a metal bowl set over a pan of simmering water. Stir frequently until melted and smooth. Remove from the heat, and stir in the shortening until melted.

2. Line a baking sheet with waxed paper. Add blueberries to the chocolate, and stir gently to coat. Spoon small clumps of blueberries onto the waxed paper. Refrigerate until firm, about 10 minutes. Store in a cool place in an airtight container. These will last about 2 days.

LIQUOR-INFUSED CHOCOLATE STRAWBERRIES
Servings: 16 | Prep: 15m | Cooks: 0m | Total: 15m

NUTRITION FACTS

Calories: 231 | Carbohydrates: 23.3g | Fat: 12.5g | Protein: 2.2g | Cholesterol: 4mg

INGREDIENTS

- 16 large fresh strawberries with leaves
- 2 tablespoons shortening
- 1/2 cup brandy-based orange liqueur (such as Grand Marnier)
- 2 tablespoons heavy cream
- 1 pound bittersweet chocolate, chopped
- 1/4 cup brandy-based orange liqueur (such as Grand Marnier)
- 1 (1 ounce) square chopped white chocolate

DIRECTIONS

1. Rinse strawberries and dry thoroughly. Use a syringe or clean marinade injector to inject about 2 teaspoons of brandy into each berry. Place them on a baking sheet, and refrigerate for about 30 minutes.

2. In a metal bowl over a pan of simmering water, combine bittersweet chocolate and shortening. Stir occasionally until melted and smooth. Stir in heavy cream and 1/4 cup of brandy. Place white chocolate in a separate bowl, and when the dark chocolate has melted, place the bowl of white chocolate over the pan of simmering water, stirring occasionally until smooth. Be sure to remove from heat as soon as it is mostly melted, white chocolate can be sensitive.

3. Dip strawberries into chocolate, and let the excess drip off into the bowl before placing on waxed paper to set. When the strawberries have all been dipped in chocolate, dip a fork into the white chocolate, and drizzle back and forth over berries to stripe.

TURTLES CANDY
Servings: 24 | Prep: 15m | Cooks: 15m | Total: 8h

NUTRITION FACTS

Calories: 106 | Carbohydrates: 12.8g | Fat: 6.5g | Protein: 1.2g | Cholesterol: <1mg

INGREDIENTS

- 72 pecan halves
- 24 individually wrapped caramels, unwrapped
- 1 cup semisweet chocolate chips
- 2 teaspoons shortening

DIRECTIONS

1. Preheat oven to 300 degrees F (150 degrees C). Grease baking sheets.
2. Place three pecan halves in a Y shape on cookie sheet and place caramel in center. Repeat with remaining nuts and caramels.
3. Place in preheated oven 10 minutes, until caramel is melted.
4. Melt chocolate chips with shortening in microwave, or in a small saucepan over low heat; stir until smooth. Spoon over candies on sheets. Chill 8 hours or overnight, until firm.

MICROWAVE PECAN BRITTLE
Servings: 10 | Prep: 10m | Cooks: 9m | Total: 49m

NUTRITION FACTS

Calories: 217 | Carbohydrates: 34.3g | Fat: 9.7g | Protein: 1.1g | Cholesterol: 3mg

INGREDIENTS

- 1 cup chopped pecans
- 1 cup white sugar
- 1/2 cup light corn syrup
- 1/8 teaspoon salt
- 1 tablespoon butter
- 1 teaspoon baking soda
- 1 teaspoon vanilla extract

DIRECTIONS

1. Butter a baking sheet.
2. Combine pecans, sugar, corn syrup, and salt in a glass 4-cup measuring cup.
3. Heat in microwave for 3 1/2 minutes; stir and heat for 3 1/2 more minutes. Stir butter into pecan mixture and heat in microwave for 2 more minutes.

4. Stir baking soda and vanilla extract into pecan mixture until foamy; pour onto the prepared baking sheet. Allow to cool completely before breaking brittle into pieces. Store in an airtight container.

BAKED FUDGE
Servings: 12 | Prep: 10m | Cooks: 1h | Total: 1h10m

NUTRITION FACTS

Calories: 380 | Carbohydrates: 40.7g | Fat: 24.1g | Protein: 4.3g | Cholesterol: 102mg

INGREDIENTS

- 2 cups white sugar
- 1/2 cup all-purpose flour
- 1/2 cup unsweetened cocoa powder
- 4 eggs, beaten
- 1 cup butter, melted
- 2 teaspoons vanilla extract
- 1 cup chopped pecans

DIRECTIONS

1. Preheat oven to 300 degrees F (150 degrees C).
2. In large bowl, sift together sugar, flour and cocoa. Add eggs. Add melted butter, vanilla and pecans. Pour mixture into 8x12-inch baking pan.
3. Line a roasting pan with a damp kitchen towel. Place baking dish on towel, inside roasting pan, and place roasting pan on oven rack. Fill roasting pan with boiling water to reach halfway up the sides of the baking dish. Bake 50 to 60 minutes or until firm.

CARROT RECIPE
Servings: 4 | Prep: 5m | Cooks: 12m | Total: 17m

NUTRITION FACTS

Calories: 486 | Carbohydrates: 88.3g | Fat: 13.6g | Protein: 8.4g | Cholesterol: 17mg

INGREDIENTS

- 4 cups grated carrots
- 1 tablespoon butter
- 2 cups milk
- 1/2 cup cashew halves

- 1 cup white sugar
- 1/2 cup raisins
- 1 pinch ground cardamom (optional)

DIRECTIONS

1. In a saucepan over medium heat, combine carrots and milk. Bring to a boil, and cook until most of the milk evaporates, about 10 minutes. Stir in sugar, and simmer until mixture becomes dry. Stir constantly to ensure that it doesn't burn. Remove from heat.

2. Melt butter in a skillet over medium heat. Stir in cashews and raisins, and saute until cashews are golden brown. Spread over carrot mixture. Sprinkle top with ground cardamom for fragrance.

Made in the USA
Middletown, DE
14 April 2023

28872322R00051